EXTRAORDINARY
RESULTS

*Mastering the Art of
Leading, Coaching, &
Influencing Others*

ALSO BY
JOE CONTRERA

*LIGHT 'EM UP!: How to Ignite the Fire
in Your Sales Team in Just 21 Days*

I Could Love No One...Until I Loved Me

EXTRAORDINARY RESULTS

Mastering the Art of Leading, Coaching, & Influencing Others

JOE CONTRERA

AWP

Copyright © 2018, Joe Contrera and ALIVE @ WORK® LLC
All rights reserved. The use of any part of this publication,
reproduced, transmitted in any form or by any means, electronic,
mechanical, photocopying, recording or otherwise stored in a
retrieval system, without the prior consent of the publisher
is an infringement of the copyright law.

ALIVE @ WORK® PUBLISHING
PO Box 94503
Phoenix, AZ 85070
sales@aliveatworkpublishing.com
1–877–972–5483
www.aliveatwork.com

Kelly Lydick, M.A., editor
David Moratto, cover and interior design

First Edition
Printed in the U.S.A.

LCCN: 2017915765
Issued in print, electronic, and audio format.
ISBN: 978-0-9747602-2-3 (hardcover).
ISBN: 978-0-9747602-1-6 (e-book).
ISBN: 978-0-9747602-3-0 (audio book).

*This book is dedicated to my mom,
Rose Amelia Adornetto Contrera,
better known as simply "Rosie."*

*Mom you are a beacon of strength,
determination, and faith.
I love you more than you will ever know
and I am proud to call you my Mom.*

I Love You Rosie!

CONTENTS

FOREWORD *1*

PART I
MASTERING THE ART OF LEADING OTHERS

CHAPTER 1: LEADING OTHERS & INFLUENCE *9*
    Simple Truth *9*
    Defining Extraordinary Leadership *10*
    Defining Influence *11*
    Defining an Extraordinary Leader Who Influences *12*

CHAPTER 2: LEADERSHIP PERSPECTIVES: POWER VS. FORCE *15*
    Power vs. Force *16*
    Leading by Influence & Authority: Power vs. Force *17*
    Focus: Other-Centered or Self-Centered? *19*
    Worldview: Friendly or Hostile? *21*
    Resources: Abundance or Scarcity? *22*
    Driven by: Trust or Fear? *24*
    Communication: Transparent or Opaque? *25*
    Conversations: Asking or Telling? *28*

EXTRAORDINARY RESULTS

Leadership View: Privilege or Entitlement? *30*
Accountability, Ownership, & Impact:
    Employee-Based or Leader-Based? *31*
Practicing the Art: Power vs. Force:
    What's your InQ (Influence Quotient)? *33*

CHAPTER 3: YOU ARE WHO YOU ARE — TAKING 100% RESPONSIBILITY *35*
Will the Real You Please Stand Up! *36*
The Underlying Issue Facing Us All *37*
Am I Enough? *39*
The Truth About You *40*

CHAPTER 4: FINDING YOUR PATH: START HERE *43*
Places to Start *43*
Outside-In: (Objective Feedback)
    Looking Outside to Better Understand the Inside *44*
Outside-In: (Subjective Feedback)
    Getting Feedback, Building Trust, & The V-Word. *47*
Inside Out. *50*
Practicing the Art: What's your AQ (Awareness Quotient)? *53*

CHAPTER 5: ARE YOU A LEADER OR A GLORIFIED INDIVIDUAL CONTRIBUTOR?. . . . *55*
The Biggest Jump You Will Ever Make *56*
Why Most Leaders Fail *57*
Your Worst Nightmare. *58*
Where Do You Stand? *59*

CHAPTER 6: LEADING AUTHENTICALLY *63*
The Relationship Between Integrity & Authenticity *64*
Being Who You Are *67*
Trusting Who You Are *68*

CHAPTER 7: LEADING FROM YOUR STRENGTHS *71*
Uncovering Your Strengths. *71*

viii

CONTENTS

Leading From Your Strengths 72
Embracing Your Strength Will Get You Engaged and... 74
Finding Your Path...Leading Others to Theirs 75

CHAPTER 8: CREATING YOUR LEADERSHIP STRATEGY 77
Don't Be a Floyd 78
Sustaining Long-Lasting Change 79
Re-Beliefing Process 79
Re-Beliefing Your Beliefs 80
The Cost of Not Changing? 83
Practicing the Art: Deciding to Be a Leader 84

PART II
MASTERING THE ART OF COACHING OTHERS

CHAPTER 9: COACHING OTHERS & INFLUENCE 91
Coaching Defined 91
Understanding Coaching & Influence 93
Defining an Extraordinary Leader Who Coaches 94
Practicing the Art: What's your CQ (Coaching Quotient)? 96

CHAPTER 10: THE A.R.T. OF THE QUESTION 97
Voltaire Was a Pretty Smart Guy 97
Questioning Your Approach 99
The Art of Questioning Others 100
More Powerful Than a Locomotive 104

CHAPTER 11: GREMLINS: MOVING THROUGH THE FEAR F.I.L.L.E.R.S.™ 107
Gremlins? Say What? 108
Gremlins and Fear 109
Overcoming Fear: The FEAR F.I.L.L.E.R.S.™ 110
Coaching Your Folks...Not Their Gremlins 115

Practicing the Art: Freedom from Fear *117*

CHAPTER 12: VICTIMHOOD & THE POWER OF CHOICE *119*
The Victim Mentality *119*
Getting Unstuck: Holding The Mirror *122*
Getting to Choices *123*
Empowering Others *127*

CHAPTER 13: ACCOUNTABILITY, PUSHBACK, & CURING THE DIS-EASE *131*
Addressing The Dis-ease...Not the Symptom *131*
Accountability and Pushback *135*
How to Place Accountability Where It Belongs *138*

CHAPTER 14: THE COACHING MINDSET *141*
To Be...or Not to Be *141*
Short-Term Cost vs. Long-Term Return *143*
The Ultimate Goal of Coaching *144*

CHAPTER 15: COACHING:
10 THINGS TO REMEMBER, 10 THINGS TO FORGET, 10 THINGS TO DO *147*
10 Things To Remember *147*
10 Things To Forget *148*
10 Things To Do *149*
Practicing the Art: Ribbon On Your Finger *151*

PART III
MASTERING THE ART OF INFLUENCING OTHERS
∞

CHAPTER 16: INFLUENCE VS. MANIPULATION *155*
Remember...It's All About the Intention *157*
Crossing the Line *158*
Influencing: Outside-In *159*

CONTENTS

Influencing: Inside-Out *159*

Practicing the Art: Clarifying Intentions *161*

CHAPTER 17: THE ART OF INFLUENCING MODEL *163*

Step 1: Defining Where You Want / Need to Be / Do / Go . . . *163*

Step 2: Defining Where You Are Right Now *164*

Step 3: Understanding Where the Individual is Right Now *165*

Step 4: Identify the Desires & the Need *167*

Step 5: Identify the Pain & the Cost *168*

Step 6: Identify the Obstacles *169*

Step 7: Identify The Actions Needed to Change / Move / Grow . . *170*

Step 8: Get Agreement, Commitment & Hold Accountable . . . *171*

Step 9: Praise / Coach / Thank / Move On *173*

The Journey of Influence *175*

Practicing the Art:

  What Have You Noticed About Others' Ability to Influence? *176*

CHAPTER 18: THE ART OF FACILITATION *177*

Coaching on Steroids *177*

It's As Easy As 1-2-3 . . . . *179*

What Could Possibly Go Wrong? *184*

CHAPTER 19: THE ART OF PAINTING THE(IR) PICTURE *187*

Tools To Create the Masterpiece *188*

CHAPTER 20: THE ART OF WASTING TIME: MEETINGS *197*

What A Lack of Planning Really Means *198*

The 5 Immutable Laws of Conducting Meetings *200*

CHAPTER 21: THE ART OF PRESENTING *205*

Painting Your Picture: Influencing 1 on 100+ *205*

Miss-takes: How Do Things Go Wrong? *206*

Getting Buy-In *207*

Power of Story: The Me–You Connection *210*

xi

S.P.A.: A Foolproof Story Formula 211
Tools to Enhance Your Masterpiece 214
Finishing Touches 221
Practicing the Art: Creating the Stories 222

SUMMARY 223
A Tale of Two Leaders 223
Your Leadership Story 225
REFERENCES 229
INDEX 235
ACKNOWLEDGEMENTS 245

FOREWORD

Years ago, I had the fortune of spending some time in Florence, Italy. During my trip to the Academia Gallery I had the opportunity to sit and take in what I believe is one of the greatest masterpieces in all of the world, Michelangelo's *David*. I could try to tell you that it is magnificent, that it is fabulous, but until you experience this work of art, I can only share my experience, which we know would be far different than yours.

With just the smallest amount of research you find that the statue was created between 1501 and 1504 and stands 17 feet in the air. It is a statue depicting David, the biblical hero who slew Goliath, the Philistine Giant with a simple sling.

As the story goes, Michelangelo was asked to complete the unfinished project that had begun 36 years earlier by two other artists, Agostino di Duccio and later Antonio Rossellino. It was well known at the time that both artists had rejected the enormous marble block because according to them, it held far too many imperfections to be usable or to achieve the desired result...and so it sat for 25 years.

Michelangelo was just 26 years old when he accepted the challenge to sculpt the *David* from this massive rock. He worked diligently for more than two years to complete this incredible task.

To sit at the feet of his work and take in the subtle detail of the bulging veins on the hands and the perfect muscular depiction of the human anatomy is indescribable.

You notice that certain parts of the body are enlarged so they can be seen from the perspective of the audience, who was originally supposed to be viewing the sculpture from 260 feet below while it was perched on top of a building. Which begs the question...why such attention to detail for a statue that was to be viewed from so far away?

As the story goes, when Michelangelo unveiled his near-complete masterpiece, it was deemed to be too perfect to be displayed in such a position. A committee of 30 members, who included the likes of Leonardo da Vinci and Sandro Botticelli, decided that the statue would be placed in the political heart of Florence, in the Piazza della Signoria on June 8th of 1504.

After moving the near-complete work to the Piazza, Michelangelo continued to perfect the intimate details that transformed this giant stone into an even more lifelike statue.

The *David* sat outside in the Piazza della Signoria from 1504 until 1873, when it was moved to the Academia. The intention was to protect it from further damage caused by being exposed to 369 years of weathering, from both natural and unnatural factors.

And yet, you can't help but see the pure brilliance and genius of the artist represented in this form, a form chiseled from what was deemed poor quality rock by lesser artists.

After being exposed to the elements for so many years, along with the dirt and dust of everyday seeping into the marble, the *David* began to show its age. There were various attempts to restore this statue to its most original state and, like most things, there were arguments between those who proposed a variety of right and proper processes by which it would be restored.

Some took a forceful approach using hydrochloric acid and iron brushes, which resulted in damaging the piece. Others used a much gentler approach, even though it was painstakingly slow and tedious. By combining distilled water and clay over handmade Japanese rice paper they drew out the dirt and then carefully removed it to reveal the inner brilliance and genius of the artist that lay hidden for all these years. Sometimes achieving extraordinary results takes time and patience.

Today, you can sit for hours and be influenced and inspired by this incredible statue. I'm not sure Michelangelo ever dreamed that his story about his decision to carve the *David* would be influencing the lives of others, or that his art would still be mesmerizing millions of people each year.

The original meaning of the word *art* was defined as a "skill, a craft, or craftsmanship." Years ago, an untrained artist or craftsman was apprenticed to a master. The apprentice then spent a minimum of two years (or longer) learning the ins and outs of mastering their craft. For example, at the age of 13, Michelangelo's father, realizing that his son had no interest in traditional schooling or the family banking business, apprenticed the young man to the master painter, Domenico Ghirlandaio, where his talent began to develop. He later studied under the master sculptor, Bertoldo di Giovanni, where he would find his true passion to sculpt.

Leading, Coaching, and Influencing Others is an art and yet when it comes to developing leaders these days, sadly we do the exact opposite of apprenticing students to teachers. Instead, we take a high-performing individual contributor who is achieving great results and promote them into a leadership position. We do this before we determine whether they have the desire to lead or whether they possess the skills and tools (the brushes if you will), to effectively lead others.

The truth is that most selected do not possess the skills needed and so they scramble and attempt to apply the same principles that made them successful as an individual contributor to their new role as a leader. The results are leaders who micromanage, over control, and do the work themselves. This creates employees who are disengaged and unmotivated because they feel underutilized and undervalued.

When they fail to achieve the results we expected, we don't own that we set these new leaders up for failure. Instead, we either blame it on the leader and remove them (losing a great individual contributor in the process), or we ignore the issue and hope it will resolve itself. It rarely does.

In order to fix the problem we send leaders to be trained. TrainingIndustry.com, which utilizes data gathered from the U.S. Bureau of Economic Analysis, estimates that U.S. companies spend approximately $161 billion a year on training. And yet, so many leaders question the overall effectiveness of those dollars spent because in many ways there is no way to measure the return on investment.

Still, organizations continue to send their leaders to half-day, one-day, and two-day workshops despite that 75% of what they are taught they forget when they walk out of the training room because there is no system in place to implement the learning or continue to build the skills. You don't achieve extraordinary results sitting in a training class for a few hours or a few days. You achieve extraordinary results over time and with practice, accountability, and an ongoing process in place to continuously hone those skills.

This book is about Mastering the Art of Leading, Coaching, and Influencing others. It is about the subtleties and the skill of leading others to do their best work, be their best selves, so they can achieve extraordinary results. The misconception about influencing others is that it falls into the category of what we call "soft skills." Many leaders believe that soft skills will not get you the results that driving people and processes forward will achieve. In fact, many leaders, especially task-driven leaders, see soft skills as a weakness. These leaders see soft skills as an obstacle to achieving results instead of a path that will achieve extraordinary results. This book will teach you how to achieve extraordinary results by leveraging the power of influence. Our 7-month Leadership Development Program, *The Art of Leading, Coaching, & Influencing Others*™ is a revolutionary way of training leaders that blends the benefits of interactive classes, executive coaching, group coaching calls, accountability programs, and an ongoing 360-degree feedback model that facilitates a life-changing process. Like the course, this book was written specifically for leaders who are driven to

FOREWORD

achieve extraordinary results. Most leaders know only one way to lead: The same way that got them success as an individual contributor. This book offers you another way. It isn't about teaching you what to do to lead, it teaches you how to be a leader.

You will learn the basic core principles of influence to achieve extraordinary results—whether you are influencing 1 on 1, 1 on 10, or 1 on 100. Master these principles, build your skills, and use them to transform your ability to influence others exponentially. The more people you can influence, the more extraordinary your results will be.

Why I Wrote This Book

I have waited more than 10 years to write this book. This book is the culmination of more than 30 years of professional development. It is everything I have learned about people and influencing others. I have learned that it doesn't really matter the situation: whether it involves sales, leading others, coaching an employee, facilitating a small group, or presenting to 1,000 people...the skills required to successfully influence others and lead teams are all the same!

This book will help you understand the theory, concepts, and relationship between Leading, Coaching, and Influencing.

Whether you are new to leadership or you have been in a leadership position for 30 years or more, there is something in this book specifically for you.

If you are holding this book in your hand, there is a very good chance that this is the perfect time for you to read it. How do I know? Because you're holding this book and nothing happens by chance.

I don't care if this is the very first leadership book you've purchased or the hundred and first, I just have one question for you:

Are you willing to do the work so that you can achieve extraordinary results?

The truth about this book is the same truth that applies to life. What you put in is what you get back. Put in a little, get a little. Put in a lot, get a lot. You can take a few ideas from the first few pages or you can learn all the way through to the very end.

The ideas you take from this book won't mean a damn thing if you don't take action and integrate those ideas into your interactions with others. It is about getting results, and you won't get results if you simply think and don't take action.

At the end of select chapters you will find a section titled *Practicing the Art*. It is written to offer questions and ideas to help you put these ideas into motion. Additionally, within some of the chapters you will find additional tools and assessments to embed these concepts into your daily leadership practice. The further you embed these concepts and ideas into who you are as a leader, the closer you get to achieving results that are extraordinary.

Becoming a leader who Masters the Art of Leading, Coaching, & Influencing Others will not happen overnight. It requires effort, commitment, and a willingness to change. It also requires the humbleness and vulnerability to fail. If you are willing to do the work, if you are willing to fail and try again, you just might find that just like Michelangelo, you, too, have significantly influenced the lives of others…and what a story that would be!

PART I
MASTERING THE ART OF LEADING OTHERS

CHAPTER 1

LEADING OTHERS & INFLUENCE

Simple Truth

People have been studying, analyzing, and attempting to define what characteristics and attributes make a great leader for thousands of years. Every few years or so a new leadership theory hits the training and personal development world and a new fad is born.

Each fad promises success, whether it be 10 Ways To Communicate Better or 5 Ways To Be More Effective. The bottom line is that there are a lot of folks trying to grab your attention and they all have the best intention to help you be a better leader, salesperson, manager, husband, or wife. That is just the way the self-improvement industry works. The hope is you will find what you need to grow in one of these books, and yet the expectation seems to be that they each hold the silver bullet that will cure all of your problems.

The simple truth is that there is no silver bullet, book, or single training event that will cure your dis-ease or your issues. Chances are, if you are struggling with an issue, you always will. You can work on it and improve in that area, but it rarely ever goes away completely.

For example, if you don't like conflict you probably never will. You can acquire skills and a mindset that may change how you face conflict that will make you more effective, but you will never like it! That's okay, you don't have to like conflict to be a great leader, you just need to effectively manage through it.

CHAPTER 1

This book is rooted in simple truths, simple ideas, and simple actions you can take to increase your ability to influence others more impactfully. Just remember simple isn't always easy, and easy isn't always simple. Things will be hard until they are not. In other words, when you decide that something isn't hard, it won't be, it will just be something you do.

Defining Extraordinary Leadership

You can argue back and forth about who you feel is a great leader. You can turn on any cable news network and watch panels of experts debate the topic of leadership and who is a good leader and who is labeled a horrible one. At times, it is difficult to comprehend how folks can hold such diametrically opposed opinions of the very same person. You love Donald Trump, you hate Donald Trump, you love Angelina Jolie, you hate Angelina Jolie. Who's right?

If I asked you, based on your experiences, to tell me about the leaders who have influenced you in a positive way, I'm sure you could mention at least one person. You might mention a person you worked for at one time, or maybe a parent or relative, a teacher or your high school soccer coach. Regardless of whom you selected, they influenced you to achieve more, to be more, or accomplish more than you thought you were capable of achieving. In the same way, I'm sure you could also bring to mind a leader that impacted or influenced you in an incredibly negative way as well.

All of us have been influenced throughout our lives by leaders — some good and some not so good. The ones we remember the most are those who had a positive influence on our lives, the ones who helped bring out the best in us — those who help us to accomplish extraordinary results.

Successful leadership comes down to your ability to influence others. In fact, the definition of a leader is exactly that:

LEADING OTHERS & INFLUENCE

A leader is a person who influences others to do or to be their best.

Based on that definition, everyone has the ability to influence others —which means in some small way every one of us has the opportunity to lead.

True leaders realize that in order to influence others to do or to be their best, they first have to stop focusing on themselves. That's easier said than done.

Why? Because most leaders got promoted to a leadership position after they had proven themselves as an individual contributor. Individual contributors succeed because they do the work themselves, and they focus their efforts on themselves and their individual contribution. They directly impact the work.

Leaders, on the other hand, have to step back and influence others to get the work done. For some leaders this is a huge problem because they don't know how to influence, they only know how to get the work done. The single biggest shift any leader has to make is the jump from being an individual contributor to being a leader. It is a complete and total shift from doing the work to having the ability to influence others to do the work without micromanaging or stepping in and taking over or doing it themselves. This is a challenge that highly driven individual contributors fall into when they don the leadership cape.

Defining Influence

Merriam-Webster's dictionary defines *influence* as "the power to change or affect someone or something." This means the power to cause changes without directly forcing them to happen. A leader, in this context then, is a person or thing that affects someone or something in an important way.

CHAPTER 1

I am often asked about the difference between influencing and manipulating others. I don't mean to generalize here but...the question usually comes from leaders who are very nice and are worried that they are being sneaky and insidious.

So, what is the difference between influence and manipulation?

Let me reframe it with a question: How many of you love the experience of sitting down across the table from a car salesperson and his "manager" to buy a car?

For most non-driver, non-type-A personality people who are not driven by a need to win, buying a car is a terrible experience because they feel like they are being manipulated. The truth is...they probably are.

Car salespeople know they have a very limited window of time to sell you a car, because they know if you walk out that door chances are you're not coming back. So they have to pull out all of the stops to get what they want...to sell you a car!

Here's how Merriam-Webster defines *manipulation*: "to manage or utilize skillfully: to control or play upon by artful, unfair, or insidious means, especially to one's own advantage." While not all car salespeople are like this, a high percentage of them are. The key here is that the difference between whether it is influence or manipulation comes down to the intention of the person who is attempting to influence. Manipulators emphasize their own advantage. Leaders emphasize what works for everyone, and put the needs of the other person first. The question then becomes: Is it a person's intention to get what they themselves need? Or is it about helping the other person get what they need?

Defining an Extraordinary Leader Who Influences

In order to be an extraordinary leader, you must truly understand the purpose behind leading. Your job as a leader is to hold up a flashlight —and sometimes a mirror—so that your team can see the obstacles

LEADING OTHERS & INFLUENCE

they are placing in their paths, tripping over, and then looking outwardly for the causes.

The job is to help the team understand that they are placing those obstacles in their path, and that they are responsible for removing those obstacles so that they can move forward. Forward can be realized as better results, a promotion, a higher level of productivity, a bonus, an increase, a job they truly want, or even a career shift that takes them away from your team, and sometimes your company. In the end, leaders help others to achieve extraordinary results.

Years ago, I was working with a company that was going through a merger. One of the leaders I was working with was terrified that his job was in jeopardy because the corporate headquarters was being moved to a different location. Operating from a fear-based mindset, he decided to withhold information as a way to become invaluable. He falsely believed that if he withheld the information and no one else had access to it, they would never get rid of him. He would be irreplaceable! You can probably see where this is going?

As a result of keeping things secretive and withholding information that would benefit the team, he and the company eventually parted ways. Why? He was viewed as someone who wasn't a team player and wasn't willing to adjust to the new culture or the changes that were taking place around him. Had he been able to see that his behavior was giving him the exact opposite results that he wanted, he might have decided to do things differently. The problem was that he was continuing to blame everyone else for his problems. If the merger had never happened, if they just kept the corporate headquarters where he was located, everything would have been fine. He pointed outward at everyone else and blamed them because he wasn't willing to take 100% responsibility for the fact that his beliefs and his actions were the root cause of his poor reviews and disciplinary actions.

Sometimes what is best for the employee is to move forward by moving away. The reality of the situation above was that deep down the employee wasn't really happy. He eventually went off and started his own business.

CHAPTER 1

Sometimes an extraordinary leader can get so wrapped up in their own needs and their own agenda, they overlook what might be best for the employee. You may get so heavily invested in holding on to an employee that wants to or needs to move on. When this happens it may mean that you do everything you can to get them to stay, and then there is a good chance your conversation will either border on manipulation or be full-blown manipulation.

Focusing on others is simple, but sometimes isn't even close to being easy. Most humans are wired to make sure we get our needs met first. Some of the greatest teachers in the world: Gandhi, Jesus, the Dalai Lama, Lao Tzu, Mother Teresa, Muhammad, Martin Luther King Jr., Buddha, believed that your path to success, happiness—and even enlightenment—begins when you can get out of your own way and focus on helping others.

Being an extraordinary leader is no different. You may not change the world but you can influence the lives of your people and those you lead in a significant way. Then again, who knows? You or one of the people you lead may just change the world in a way neither one of you could ever imagine!

CHAPTER 2
LEADERSHIP PERSPECTIVES: POWER VS. FORCE

A few years ago, I had the opportunity to work with an executive who was recently promoted. At the time he was extremely frustrated with one of his leaders. As I asked him to explain what the challenges were, he went into great detail about his attempts to constantly get this guy to "fall into line." He was astounded by the fact that the more attempts he made to apply pressure downward, the more this leader pushed back. At times it was direct, which the executive deemed as insubordination. At other times, it was very subtle: missed deadlines, absenteeism, and lack of follow up. Normally you would say, problem employee, get rid of them! The problem was that the leader was a stellar employee, highly rated by his peers and his previous director. After he explained the situation, I leaned over and asked the executive to place his hand against mine. As he did I started push on his hand and he immediately started pushing back. He wasn't going to lose the battle. I stopped pushing and said, "Newton's third law states, for every action, there is an equal and opposite reaction; now maybe you understand the situation? He is actually more like you than you think. I never asked you to push back, you simply started pushing against me; the more I pushed, the harder you pushed. So, what do you want to do now? You can either act out of your ego, and demand loyalty and respect, or you can look for a solution...your call."

CHAPTER 2

Power vs. Force

A number of years ago, a colleague of mine recommended a book titled *Power vs. Force* by David Hawkins. It was an extremely interesting book and although it pertained to applied kinesiology, quantum physics, particles, waves, and vibration, it was incredibly thought-provoking. Years later, as I was studying leadership and influence, I came to the conclusion that the entire theory of Power vs. Force could apply to leadership and a leader's ability to influence others. You can lead from a place of power, which at its core is about influence and authority, or you can attempt to lead from a place of force. What follows is a very detailed comparison of the contrast between a power-based leader and a force-based leader.

Below is a chart that shows the contrast between the two styles of leadership.

Leadership & Influence: Two Perspectives		
	Power vs.	**Force**
Lead by:	*Authority/Influence	Control
Focus:	Other-Centered	Self-Centered
Worldview:	Friendly	Hostile
Resources:	Abundance	Scarcity
Driven by:	Trust	Fear
Communication:	Transparent	Opaque
Conversations:	Questions—Ask	Statements—Tell
Leadership View:	Privilege/Calling	Entitlement
Accountability, Ownership & Impact:	Employee-Based	Leader-Based
*Authority—from the word Author c. 1300. Auctor— enlarger, founder, leader, one who causes to grow.		

Leading by Influence & Authority: Power vs. Force

Most people have a negative connotation about the word "authority." They seem to confuse authority with the word control. The word authority appeared in the early 1300s and comes from the Latin word *auctor*, which means "author." Author means enlarger, founder, and one who causes to grow. This is a far different meaning than what most people believe about authority today.

A few thousand years ago, there was a wise man, a revolutionary of sorts, who taught a new way of living that was rooted in forgiveness and love, and he changed the world. His enemies feared him and one day at an early age, his adversaries after hearing him speak asked, "Who is this man who teaches with such authority?" He spoke with authority and people were drawn to him. They were not coerced or manipulated into following him, they simply agreed with what he was saying, and so they chose to follow him. He created such a following that 2000 years later he continues to influence the lives of people all over the world. He continues to be listed as the one of the most influential leaders in the history of the world. Regardless of your religious beliefs, whether you have them or you don't doesn't matter, because that isn't the point here. The point is that Jesus was one of the most influential people who ever lived and continues to be to this present day.

Eighteen hundred or so years later, another influential leader was also changing history. Standing at the dedication of the Soldiers' National Cemetery in Gettysburg, Pennsylvania, he delivered a two-hundred-and-seventy-two-word speech in less than three minutes on November 19, 1863. This speech is referenced as one of the greatest speeches of all time, although the U.S. was drastically split in half at the time. That is less than nine tweets!

The interesting point here is that Abraham Lincoln wasn't even the main attraction that day. The keynote speaker was a gentleman by the name of Edward Everett, a well-known academic and orator of his time. Everett delivered a thirteen-thousand, six-hundred-and-seven-word speech for more than two hours! Everett who?

CHAPTER 2

Influence and authority is not a derivative of how long you speak or how many words you use. It isn't about how long you have been a leader or how many degrees you have hanging on your wall. The power of influence goes much further than words, time elapsed, or characters on a piece of paper. All great leaders lead from a place of influence and authority. They are committed to enlarging the talents and skills of others, they are committed to helping others grow. Your choice to lead from a place of power begins with your decision to lead by influence and authority. Of course, there is another option.

Russia has a history rich in dictators who practice the art of control. The contrast between Russia's style of leadership and that of the freedom-based, democratic United States was never so clear than when a wall was constructed dividing the country into two diametrically opposed halves.

While you may never have lived in East Germany or experienced what it is like to live in a communist country, it is easy to see the impact and oppression that this style of leadership imposes on a culture. Leaders who seek to control their people can have a similar impact on a person, a culture, or a company, albeit in a much subtler and less violent way.

When a leader chooses to attempt to lead from a position of control, it usually doesn't end well. In the world we usually refer to these types of leaders as dictators and the world is filled with them. In the context of the workplace, we usually refer to these people as micromanagers, although I've met a few leaders in the workplace that were referred to as dictators. The fatal flaw in this style of leadership is the basic fact that most people (especially talented ones) do not like to be controlled. Most folks want to feel like they have some sense of autonomy in their work and that they are empowered to make choices. We refer to this as the locus-of-control. Leaders who are focused on keeping the locus-of-control within their own realm are usually poor at delegating, overstep their boundaries, and have a low level of trust of others. This is why they attempt (yes attempt!) to control the behaviors of their people. In most cases, behind the dictatorial bravado

18

is an internal fear that they are projecting outwardly on others. You may find a lot of drama and discourse surrounding these leaders or it may linger underneath the surface as a quiet discontentment or contempt that leaks out passive-aggressively in the workplace.

Next time you are with someone, ask them to hold up their hand palm facing you. Place your hand against theirs and start pushing against them. Observe what happens. Without a word spoken they will start pushing back on you as if a universal law of physics was playing out. Actually it is, it's Newton's Third Law of Motion, which states, "For every action, there is an *equal and opposite reaction.*"

When I lead by force, I exert force on you in an attempt to control you, and you will always find a way to push back. It may be outwardly in a direct and aggressive way. It may be inwardly in a passive manner that shows up as disengagement, absenteeism, playing small and shutting down. It may be hidden below the surface in a passive-aggressive way by attempting to give you a false sense of agreement, or talking behind your back, for instance. In any case, your effort to control will cause you to actually lose control. You may not see it, but you will feel it, and you will react by turning up the control knob to compensate for the loss of control...and the cycle continues...just spinning a little faster now.

Focus: Other-Centered vs. Self-Centered?

When a leader is other-centered, they make the people they interact with — their employees, their peers, their leaders — the focus of their attention. When this happens, they get a sense that your focus and energy is directed toward supporting them, and as a result they grow and develop. They trust you and so they follow you because they believe that you have their best interests in mind. That said, it is important to clarify that being a leader who is other-centered doesn't mean you coddle, overprotect them, or take responsibility for them. It means you hold them accountable because you are responsible *to* them, not

CHAPTER 2

for them. You help them to get out of their own way by helping them to find their own solutions to their problems and challenges. They learn to think for themselves—and as a result they grow. When they're growing, they're increasing their value because they're doing better work. In the end, you will get your needs met, which as a leader means that you achieve higher levels of productivity more consistently than you ever could as an individual contributor.

When a leader chooses to be self-centered, their team will sense that as well. It doesn't matter how eloquently worded their phrases or gestures are, how well they can use bravado, because it is just a matter of time until their true agenda comes to light. Politicians are notorious for attempting to make you believe that something is true when it isn't. Regardless of their words, they are focused more on themselves and being reelected, than what is best for the *American people*.

If you are a self-centered leader, people will eventually come to the realization that they don't matter and that you consistently put your needs before theirs. This starts an avalanche of problems. First, the good talent will leave because they don't trust you; they will believe that when push comes to shove they will be the ones pushed out of the way so you can take care of yourself. Second, the poor performers who are not invested in the company or their work will stay because to them it is just a j-o-b, and they couldn't care less. This combination can cost a company thousands and thousands of dollars in lost productivity.

At some point in time, we all will or have already worked for a self-centered leader. They are the ones who took credit for your work, and self-promoted themselves in front of others—especially upper management. The funny thing about them is that while they believe no one sees through the facade, the reality is quite different. The best analogy I can share here is what happens when you are driving a car and then decide to let go of the steering wheel. You don't crash immediately; no matter how hard you try or desire to not crash, it's just a matter of time before eventually you crash.

Worldview: Friendly or Hostile?

Albert Einstein once said, *"The most important decision we make is whether we believe we live in a friendly or hostile universe."* In other words, you have to decide if this place you inhabit is a safe place or a dangerous one. This means either a place where you approach each interaction with a self-protective mindset, or a place where you can relax and trust the process.

Experience, along with our upbringing, play an important role in how we pass through our days on earth. When, where, how, and by whom you were raised has an enormous impact on what is understand to be "normal."

Definitions of "normal" vary widely from person to person, family to family, and culture to culture. For example, people raised during The Great Depression of the 1930s see the world much differently than children raised in the economic boom cycle of the 1990s.

In our interconnected, multicultural world, the culture in which we were raised significantly impacts how we lead. In organizations with locations scattered all over the world, it is quite typical that as part of their leadership development program, they transfer leaders between the different countries so they can broaden their perspectives and expose them to different cultures.

I once worked with a leader from South America who struggled with conflict because in his town growing up, conflict would literally cost you your life. So he learned not to confront others (including his ·people) on performance issues or anything that resembled a conflict. His cultural background manifested itself in his desire to make everyone happy and to not make waves. The results: his employees pushed back on him, disrespected his authority, and had no accountability or ownership for their work, all of which reflected poorly upon him as a leader.

When you take into consideration the constant barrage by a news media who peddles fear and sensationalizes the facts, add the social media factor and the ability to share violent and horrific videos live, it can be extremely difficult to not be overrun by a fear-based mindset.

CHAPTER 2

For the record, I understand that the world is not all sunshine, rainbows, and unicorns. It can be difficult to maintain a positive outlook in the onslaught of what's wrong in the world. And yet, as a leader, if you choose to see that for the most part the world is a friendly place and people are good, more times than not, you will give others the benefit of the doubt. You will realize that not everyone is out to get you, make you look bad, or throw you under the bus...and you will be happier.

As a leader, when you trust others you delegate more and you micromanage less. When the world is a friendly place, you collaborate more with your people and your peers. Your ability to collaborate will allow you to get more things done than you ever could if you were isolated and hiding behind a fear-based shield. And when you get more things done, you increase your value to the organization and therefore your ability to be promoted.

In the end...you win.

If you believe the world is a friendly place, there will be times when things don't go as planned and you may occasionally get burned. In those situations, you're more likely to search for solutions and ways to make it better than to point a finger, blame, and condemn, in order to protect yourself.

Each day you have the opportunity to choose between whether you live in a friendly or hostile universe.

Maybe old Albert had it right when he said...this truly is one of the most important decisions we make.

Resources: Abundance or Scarcity?

In line with (but slightly different from) the previous perspective is whether or not you come from a place of abundance or a place of scarcity. This decision will impact your ability to lead others because it is associated indirectly with your ability to overcome adversity, perceive growth opportunities, and manage risk.

My mother is 87 years old, she grew up during the depression and although she lives alone, she still has two refrigerator freezers and one full-size freezer in the house. All three of them are over-stuffed with 3 lb. packages of pepperoncinis, pickles, and pepperoni that have expiration dates from...well let's just say a while ago.

She got upset when I told her I was going to remove her from my Costco card and told me not to worry she would get her own! Did I mention she already had her own Sam's Club card?

Like many people who were raised in the Depression, she was imprinted with a scarcity mentality. The point is that her beliefs about resources, which she was imprinted with 78 years earlier as a child, are still impacting her decisions and how she navigates the world today. There is or will never be enough of anything, food, money, opportunity, success, etc. It's not bad, it's not wrong, it just is. Can you think about a belief you were imprinted with as a child that is still impacting your decision-making or worldview?

So what does this have to do with leadership? Leaders who are scarcity-based are less willing to take risks. They operate from a place of "better to keep what we have than risk losing it all." They hold onto poor-performers far longer than they should because they believe in the old-saying, "better to work with the devil you know, than the devil you don't." They play it safe with their people and have a tendency to be frugal with their time, energy, and resources. They may make poor business decisions because they are penny-wise and pound-foolish when it comes to things like training, and they don't want to lay out the investment for something that isn't a piece of equipment. These types of leaders often fail to understand or comprehend the return on investment so they only go with the cheapest or what they've always done despite that they aren't getting the results they want because the return is more difficult to quantify. They weren't born with a scarcity mentality, they developed it from the experiences and imprinting they had along the way.

Leaders who believe that resources are abundant believe that there is enough to go around. They invest wisely and they understand

CHAPTER 2

the business is really all about managing risk. They don't make foolish decisions and when they make a decision that didn't turn out as they planned, they don't allow that to paralyze them for the rest of their lives. They make the best decision possible after they have done their homework and then they move forward until it is a better decision to change direction. A study based on ten years of research on a database of 17,000 C-Suite executives in ghSmart's Genome Project, which included more than 2,000 CEOs, revealed that two of the four behaviors found in successful CEOs were: a) deciding with speed and conviction; and b) adapting proactively to a rapidly changing environment. You cannot execute either of these if you are paralyzed in a scarcity-based mentality. You can't hold off making important decisions and watch as the window of opportunity passes by your front door. Which leads us to our next facet...

Driven by: Trust or Fear?

Someone once said when you boil it all down, you either make your decisions from a place of love or a place of fear. While this may not seem appropriate in a workplace environment, I think that you can safely say that all of us make decisions from a place of trust or fear. When you trust yourself and you trust others, you are less afraid and give most people the benefit of the doubt. Of course, there may be times when you made what you thought was a good decision. You trusted someone, whether it was an employee, your boss, or even a customer, and it came back and bit you in the ass. Maybe it was a painful lesson financially or it negatively impacted your career. After it happened, you promised yourself you would never trust anyone again. That experience could either be a valuable lesson learned, or it can be a legal precedent for how you go through the rest of your life. You have a choice.

You can trust that some people will make poor decisions, but not all make poor decisions. Some people believe that building trusts takes time. That said, I know married couples who have been married for

24

thirty years and don't trust each other to save their souls. Trust actually becomes a matter of vulnerability, and you won't make yourself vulnerable if you don't trust others or believe that the world is a hostile place. Again, we're not talking about laying yourself out to get steamrolled by less-than-trustworthy people, we're talking about an overall sense of trusting others.

From a leadership perspective, leaders who do not trust their team will have a tendency to micromanage them. They will not delegate because they feel that the other person can't do it the exact same way they would or isn't capable of getting it done at all. The problem with not being able to delegate as a leader is that you don't scale. You may be able to micromanage 10 or 20 people, but you can't micromanage 100 or 200 of them. If you attempt to do everything yourself and choose not to delegate, your ability to do more with more people will diminish greatly. And if you don't scale as a leader you are less likely to be promoted.

Leaders who trust don't do it blindly, however, they are willing to take the risks to make themselves vulnerable and trust people a little at a time. They realize that while not everyone will do things exactly the same way, they allow people the flexibility to do it the way they want or need to get it done. Leaders who trust believe that people are attempting to do their best. They might not be able to see how they're getting in their own way, but that is the job of the leader, to help others see where they're stepping on themselves. They trust in their own abilities and they trust in the abilities of their team to get the job done. They also know that when they trust others, it may make them vulnerable to failure, but that the upside of trusting their team outweighs the downside of not trusting their people a hundred times over. Their career depends on it!

Communication: Transparent or Opaque?

Transparency — *the quality or state of being free from pretense or deceit.*
Opaqueness — *attempt to block, making something hard to understand or see.*

CHAPTER 2

Much can be said about these topics because they impact every aspect of our lives. Whether it is politics, the news media, your partner or spouse, or yourself, every area of life is impacted in either a positive or negative way based on the choice to be transparent or to be opaque.

As an extraordinary leader, if I intentionally and purposely set out to deceive you or block you from seeing the truth (the facts), then I am attempting to manipulate you. Being opaque is simply an attempt to make things appear to be something other than what they are, and it is usually being driven by a self-centered agenda. It might be driven by a desire to:

- Maintain control;
- Manipulate or deceive another party in an attempt to benefit themselves (usually at the cost of the other party);
- Hide their missteps or indiscretions;
- Make something appear to be something other than what it is (facts versus fiction);
- Hide their selves so their true motives are hidden.

I remember a business transaction with someone who thought that leaving out some of the facts (lying by omission) was "okay." According to this person, they didn't lie...they didn't want me to be overly stressed about the riskiness of the transaction, so they made a decision to withhold some pertinent information that would have shifted the way I approached the business.

The Truth: I never asked to be protected, I never asked to be lied to, in fact I made it crystal clear that I wanted the facts regarding the upside and the downside of the deal. Apparently they felt like Jack Nicholson in the movie, *A Few Good Men,* when Nicholson screams back at the attorney played by Tom Cruise: "You can't handle the truth!"

Which raises the question: Why would someone decide for another what they can or cannot handle? Does it benefit anyone to decide for another if they should hear or see the facts, some of the facts, or none of the facts? It becomes problematic when another has been shielded from the truth because it is more about them getting what they want.

Truth looks like:

- In life there are winners and losers and losing sucks. Pretending everyone wins is a lie;
- He who yells the loudest and points the biggest finger usually has more to hide than the person they are accusing. Screaming and yelling is just a diversion away from themselves. Think about that next time you watch the news or a politician condemning the other party;
- Nothing is free, you end up paying for it one way or another and sometimes that "freebie" will rob you of your sense of self-worth, value, and your sense of purpose;
- When you feel entitled to things you haven't earned, you stay stuck and dependent on others. Eventually this will rob you of your self-worth, value, and sense of purpose. You can scream about it (see point #2, above) or just remember that you have the power to change;
- There are consequences for each and every action that you take or don't take. It is the Universal Law of Compensation... you cannot outsmart, outrun, or outmaneuver it!;
- What you put out there is what eventually comes back around to you.

As a leader, it is not your job to decide for others what they can handle or not handle when it comes to speaking the truth, especially if it directly impacts them. I understand the need for discretion, especially in a leadership position with knowledge that is not to be made public. I'm not talking about that situation. I'm talking about speaking the truth and being transparent so that people can decide for themselves what is their best course of action and not have someone else decide for them. For example, avoiding a tough conversation regarding performance because you are uncomfortable with conflict is doing a great disservice to your employee.

Opaqueness creates a false, egocentric mentality that you have the power to decide for others what is best for them. Opaqueness can contribute to low self-esteem and low self-worth because it creates a false sense of reality. Opaqueness depletes trust and people don't follow leaders they don't trust.

Transparency allows others to make the decision as to what is best for them, and decision-making is empowering. Feeling empowered builds self-worth and value, and reduces that sense of helplessness and victimhood. Transparency, although it can be difficult at times, creates vulnerability, and vulnerability creates trust. People follow leaders they trust.

As an extraordinary leader, each and every day you have the opportunity to choose to be opaque or transparent.

Part of being an extraordinary leader is trusting that your team is capable of making their own decisions and creating their own solutions to their problems and challenges. An extraordinary leader can't do that by shrouding the truth, the reality, or by being so self-centered that it appears they believe they're more important than their team.

Conversations: Asking or Telling?

When a leader interacts with others from a place of power, they become adept at asking great questions. The interesting fact is that most leaders feel the need to speak more than they listen. They believe that they must tell and make statements, instead of asking questions. Leaders must be able to understand the other person before attempting to be understood. Of course this requires a bit of humility and for a leader to put others first. However, there are a couple of other reasons that make even more sense for a leader to ask instead of tell.

When it comes to influencing others, the way the brain processes information comes into play because there is a big difference between what happens in the brain when someone is listening and being spoken at or to, and when the brain is engaged in answering a question.

When I am speaking to you, your brain is interpreting the meaning of those words according to your belief system and what you make things mean. As you are processing my words there is a much greater opportunity for you to interpret them in a way that is quite different than mine. Think about the game "Telephone" when someone gets a phrase and then they whisper it to the next person and then the next, and the next. By the time it gets to the last person, the message can be completely distorted. A muskrat can easily become Manitowoc in a matter of minutes. The second thing that can happen is that you disengage because you don't need to be engaged, especially if you are ignoring, faking listening, or going down your own thought process completely unbeknownst and separately from me.

When I am asking you a question, it causes your brain to focus in on one topic, the topic I am asking you to explain or share your insights on. I am gaining insight into what you believe about a particular situation or topic. Once I understand how you think about a particular topic, I am able to see and understand where the gaps are between where you are on a particular topic and where I am. When I have this knowledge, I am better prepared to discuss how we might close that gap so we are more aligned. We will talk about this a little more in detail later in the book.

The goal of having a conversation isn't that your people sit at the feet of the great and almighty wizard, although I have seen this behavior exhibited many times. It is the same behavior you see exhibited in a public place when a person with a cell phone is speaking loudly so everyone can hear in the hopes that people will see them as important. In actuality they see them as an ego-centric jackass who thinks everybody wants to hear what they have to say. By asking questions, I help you to come up with your own solutions to your challenges. I can still guide you, but I do it with questions rather than answers and information. Yes, there will be times when I need to share information, but predominantly the role of a leader is to develop folks and teach them how to think, not tell them what to do. Voltaire said, "Judge a man by his questions rather than his answers." An entire chapter is devoted to The Art of Asking Great Questions, Chapter 10.

CHAPTER 2

Leadership View: Privilege or Entitlement?

When you look at how most companies select leaders, it is a rather simple process.

We take an individual contributor who is a great performer (because they achieved great results), offer them more money, a more prestigious title, and a bigger office or cubicle. We don't always have a great vetting process in place because we are in a hurry, so we end up putting a body in a position instead of a person with a true desire to lead. A survey conducted by Development Dimensions International Inc. of more than 1,100 leaders across the United States said that more than fifty percent of managers took their promotion for the increase in compensation. The hope in selecting this high performer is that as a new leader they will achieve the same results they did as an individual contributor...only times ten.

If we don't offer leadership training and we assume the leader will develop their leadership skills on their own, we magnify the problem. We may assume they already know how to Lead, Coach, and Influence Others, or that they will learn on their own and figure it all out on their own. The negative impact of all of these decisions, however, may not surface until months or even years down the road.

The worst possible outcome of a poorly trained leader who doesn't understand that being a leader is a privilege occurs when the leader feels that they are qualified to lead simply because they were successful as an individual contributor and have earned their stripes. This belief leads to a foundational disconnect to the true meaning of the word leader. It is also the most ineffective style of leadership because it implies that "I am qualified to lead and my title commands that you do what I say." This can be seen in organizations all over the world, and is more prevalent in family businesses where the son or daughter is next in line to lead, regardless of their experience or qualifications. The current leadership in North Korea is a perfect example of this concept and exemplifies the true devastation of an entitled leader.

If you hold the pseudo-belief that you can control others just based on your title or position—you're in for a big surprise. If you believe people will follow you or must follow you because of your title or position—you're in for an *even bigger* surprise.

These types of managers or supervisors don't understand that leadership is truly a privilege. They fail to understand that the true job of a leader is to develop their team as individuals. It isn't about doing the work themselves...*it is* about influencing their team to do the work and to get the work done through their team—not over or around them. Telling them what to do will not work, but guiding them and using The Art of Leading, Coaching, and Influencing, and asking great questions can work. Scalability is the ability to scale up to the level of work and the results which you are responsible for delivering. The higher you go, the greater the expectation and the greater the results you must deliver. And you can't do that on your own. You have to leverage all of your talent through all of your team members and get them to perform at their highest level. If your team doesn't trust you, and if they believe that your leadership is all about you and not about them, you simply won't scale up to the next level.

When you come to the realization that being entrusted with the weight and responsibility of developing people and bringing out the best in them, you will realize that being a leader is not easy! At times it may be the most difficult thing you have ever done in your life besides raising your children. It requires dedication and a commitment: a commitment so strong that you have to lean in so far that you can't go back. It means that if you don't feel called to be a leader, you will not weather the storms very well when they arrive. And storms always occur. If you don't feel called to be a leader, then I don't suggest that you follow the path to leadership.

Accountability, Ownership, & Impact: Employee-Based or Leader-Based?

A lot of research has been done on the topic of employee engagement. One of the components that determines the level of engagement is locus-of-control. This refers to who holds the accountability, owner-ship, and impact of the work.

The successful companies and organizations are those that place accountability, ownership, and impact at the employee level.

Here's why:

Leader-Based: When accountability, ownership, and impact are held at the leadership level, it is more about the leader and their desire to control the process and the employees. It means that the leader holds the keys to the kingdom and the project or work revolves around them. It can show up as micromanaging, attempts to control the be-haviors of their people, or grandstanding, especially in meetings with the next level of leadership. The problem is that it reduces the level of ownership and responsibility in the employees and the team. Employ-ees may feel like pawns on a chessboard being moved from task to task in response to the commands of the leader. And because they are simply doing what they're told, they have a tendency to disengage instead of being fully engaged in meaningful work. Leaders who lead from this perspective are more apt to say it was a team effort, but act as if they themselves are the reason the team succeeded, especially when it comes time to share the credit.

Employee-Based: When accountability, ownership, and impact are held at the employee level, employees are more engaged. They feel that their work is important and they can make a real difference in the outcome. They are more apt to offer suggestions and push themselves because they know they are responsible for finding solutions and bringing the project in on time and within budget. Ideas flow a little freer because they know that the leader is looking to them to create solutions instead of worrying about offending a leader who feels as if they know best, or that only they have the best ideas. The latest research by Google shows that the freedom to share their ideas and suggestions without retribution or criticism (psychological safety) is the most important characteristic of a successful team.

Allowing accountability, ownership, and impact is important especially with younger employees (millennials). They need to come to work and feel like they have a say in their work and that they can make a difference. The days of blindly following a leader are passing. This reality has even forced the United States Marine Corps to revamp their training. Why? Because they realized that wars are fought differently today than they were twenty years ago. Service members today, at times, need to make decisions on their own in the moment. They also realized that the recruits enlisting today are much different than the ones who enlisted fifteen or twenty years ago. The world is changing and so leaders need to change in order to stay relevant.

You can lead from a place of power, or you can lead from a place of force. The decision is yours, and so are the consequences.

Practicing the Art:
Power vs. Force: What's your InQ (Influence Quotient)?

Understanding your relationship to Power and Force is a key indicator of your ability to effectively influence others. While most leaders have a pretty high assessment of themselves, a self-evaluation is a great place to start to uncover your strengths. To find out your place on the Power vs. Force continuum visit: www.aliveatwork.com/assessments and select the Influence Quotient (InQ) to take the assessment. You will need to enter your name and email address. Once you take the assessment, you will receive your results shortly thereafter, along with a few ideas on how to advance your leadership abilities and become more influential.

CHAPTER 3
YOU ARE WHO YOU ARE— TAKING 100% RESPONSIBILITY

If you intend to be an extraordinary, influential leader, you must be willing to take a thorough inventory of yourself and be responsible for the results of that inventory. For some, this is easy because they enjoy learning about themselves. In fact, they are their most favorite topic and they read like an open book; it's almost as if you know more than you really want to know about them. These are the extroverts and they thrive on the experience of meeting new people and trying new and exciting things.

Then we find the quiet, more introverted folks who are less likely to wear their emotions on their sleeves, are more reserved, and speak when it is necessary or after they have thought through what they intended to say. These are the folks that can have conversations and be social, although it is a draining experience. While I am generalizing between two extremes, the fact is we all lie somewhere between the two endpoints. It doesn't matter where you lie...whether you lean toward the introverted side or the extroverted side, even though there is a general belief that extroverts make better leaders. Not true, they are just louder, get noticed more, and don't have a problem telling people about themselves or what needs to be done.

Owning 100% of who you are is critically important if you are going to take 100% responsibility for your work, yourself, and your leadership abilities. It is far better to accept who you are than to attempt to change and be someone you are not. Besides, the consequences for being someone you are not are steep. You either revert back to who you are and dislike yourself for it, or you spend your life being fake and end up disliking yourself for the same reason. The truth is many of us are running around trying to be someone we're not so we can get a sense of feeling like we belong to the human race.

Will the Real You Please Stand Up!

I was working with a leader who was an IT executive. One day we were discussing how he interacted with his team and whether he came from a position of asking great questions, or whether he spent the majority of time making statements, giving advice, and providing the solutions to his team's problems. At one point, he got extremely defensive and felt that I was trying to change who he was as a person. He went on to tell me that he had been quite successful to this point in his career and had been promoted numerous times.

I mentioned to him that while that was true, his ability to scale beyond his current level of leadership was being thwarted because of his inability to lead a large number of people. He was heavily invested in always being the smartest guy in the room and needed to have all the answers. That's great if you're an individual contributor, it's not so great if you're trying to be an extraordinary leader. Being an extraordinary leader means you no longer do the work or have to be in the weeds to get the work done. Your job as a leader is to influence others to get the work done. In order to step back and make room for your team to step up and into the work, you have to be crystal clear about where you get in the way. This means where you get in the way of your team and their job, and how you get in your own way to prevent yourself from actually leading. You can't do that unless you know yourself inside and out, own how you impact others, and most importantly...take 100% responsibility for the results you are creating in your life.

The Underlying Issue Facing Us All

Chapter 2 discussed the idea of being other-centered versus being self-centered. Recall that leaders who are great influencers put the focus on others first, knowing they will get their needs met eventually and more often if they do that.

Taking 100% responsibility for the results you're creating in your life is the only time that you'll need to seriously make it about you. You probably have people that work for you or who are in your life that no matter what is happening in their lives it is or never has been their fault. They could have been in seven failed marriages and somehow it has never been their fault other than maybe that they picked the wrong person—but that was because the other person didn't show their true colors until after they were married.

When things are going wrong in my business or my life, I have to stop, review the evidence, and ask myself the critical question: Who has been at the scene of the crime in every incident? It doesn't take a rocket scientist or a detective to see that in each and every situation… it is I, myself, moi, yo, mich, and nobody else but ME!

This perception of being a victim and blaming all of one's problems on everyone or everything else is prevalent in our society. And, the unwillingness to take responsibility for ourselves, our actions, and the work we produce is showing up in the workplace more and more often. We are teaching our children that there are no consequences, that nobody loses because we never keep score, and everyone still gets a trophy. It is at best an allergic reaction and in its worst form, a full-blown disease. Like most diseases, left untreated it can be terminal. You will learn more about this in Part II, Mastering the Art of Coaching, but for now let's keep it with you.

Once you can accept that you are 100% responsible for what is unfolding in your business and your life, you've jumped over the second hurdle. Yes, the second hurdle is taking 100% responsibility for your life. The first hurdle is letting go of the concept or idea that you are perfect or that perfection can be reached. It means that you drop the facade that you project externally to everyone else (your tribe) that you are perfect and you never make mistakes, all the while internally beating the hell out of yourself with the self-talk and the gremlins you've been carrying around in your head since you were a kid. It means you stop beating yourself up, start working on self-improvement or personal growth, and start having a little grace for yourself.

I have been leading, coaching, and teaching people for more than three decades and I believe this now more than ever. It has taken me decades to come to this realization and it took seeing this pattern in companies all over the world. It was a belief that was imprinted on my brain at an early age and stayed hidden for years because it was sub-planted in an area I was unable to see at first. But when something appears at the scene of every crime, over and over again...you eventually take notice.

At the heart of everyone is a question that lies close to the heart of who they are. At times it leaks out in interactions with others, in a detrimental way, at other times it sits on their shoulder and screams in their ear when they are alone with their thoughts. It gets triggered especially in situations that involve family members, especially parents. It is the question of...AM I ENOUGH?

You could say, "No not me, I never have those thoughts. Look at what I have accomplished, I am successful, I have built a business from scratch, I have been promoted five times, I am the CIO, CEO, President of a Fortune 500 Company, I am the perfect spouse, I love my kids, and so that proves I am enough!"

Don't kid yourself—at some point we all doubt ourselves. In one way, shape, or form, we wonder if we are truly enough. This idea of not being enough is sneaky and can shift its shape so that it appears to be disguised from what it really is: fear. It may hide behind our wall of trophies and successes. It can show up in our constant and incessant striving for more. More success, more money, more adoration, or that never-ending pursuit of the illusive perfection that will finally prove that we are enough. As leaders sometimes this "not enough" mentality materializes in the bar that we hold so high for ourselves and our people, that no-thing is ever good enough.

The difference is that this "not enough" mentality can do one of three things:

- It can paralyze you and stop you from trying something new or taking action.
- It can drive you to strive to always do better. Some folks are afraid to let go of it for fear of being seen as lazy. This is predominantly a baby-boomer mindset.
- You can learn to understand the why behind it and then manage it in a way that builds you up instead of tearing you down.

Am I Enough?

In his book, *The Six Pillars of Self-Esteem,* Nathaniel Branden speaks to this idea by breaking down self-esteem into two components. The first is self-efficacy, which has been defined by psychologist Albert Bandura as one's belief in one's ability to succeed in specific situations or accomplish a task. He goes on to say that one's sense of self-efficacy can play a major role in how one approaches goals, tasks, and challenges, which means someone who is driven and has a strong sense of self-efficacy can accomplish great things.

Branden says that the second component of self-esteem has to do with the concept of self-worth and value; it has to do with the question: Am I enough? It also has a lot to do with your level of true happiness. Not the fleeting rush of a new car, promotion, raise, or suit, but the genuine happiness in knowing you are valued and appreciated. This will be a central theme in your ability to understand how to influence others, discussed later in the book.

So, you can have a high level of self-efficacy *and* be driven to succeed and achieve higher, faster, bigger, more. Now for those of you who are high achievers who are stomping your foot down because you

CHAPTER 3

may think I am saying stop achieving, stop being driven, I'm not. What I am saying is that if you are trying to leverage your self-efficacy gene to prove your self-worth from the external environment you will never succeed. Why? Because self-worth and value must come from inside of you and it is rooted in your ability to be aware of who you are (facts, not fiction or the story you've created), accept yourself, take 100% responsibility for yourself, and move forward with a sense of purpose, integrity, and action.

It is a process, not an endgame, and it doesn't happen overnight because you read this book, any other book, took a class, had an epiphany, or have a PhD.

The Truth About You

If you remember anything from this section of the book, I hope that you will remember this idea: You started in this world on the day you were born with an absolutely clean slate. As a newborn you were enough. You didn't have to do anything except be who you were. In his book, *The Four Agreements*, Don Miguel Ruiz talks about the domestication process of people. He says that just like animals, we are domesticated and imprinted with beliefs and ideas when we are younger, and these beliefs shape the way we see ourselves and the world for the rest of our lives. How we navigate through this world and the choices we make are rooted in the beliefs we were imprinted with in our formative years.

In an effort to be accepted and approved of, we go outside of ourselves and seek approval from our parents, teachers, priests, rabbis, or managers. We learn that we are not okay or enough unless folks outside of ourselves give us the thumbs up.

As we grow we either keep, reject, or change these beliefs as we add more experiences and learn new ways of doing things that can improve the results we are getting. This is why if you have teenagers in your house you are experiencing their first major phase in which they start to question the beliefs you taught them as a child.

YOU ARE WHO YOU ARE—TAKING 100% RESPONSIBILITY

In my case, I was taught that if I accomplished things that were difficult, that those things had value. I translated this into the belief that if what I did had value, then I had value. While this may sound crazy to an adult, it was what I made things mean as a child. And as children we want to be valued, and so we do the things that get us to be valued in the eyes of our parents because we equate value with being loved.

So, how does this impact me now? Later in life I found myself unconsciously making things harder than they needed to be so that I could keep proving that I was enough. One of the ways I did this was to sabotage myself and create hardships that I didn't need to create. Another way this played out was that I created a lot of drama around simple things, thinking that others would recognize how hard I was working. Sound crazy? You'd be surprised at just how many people I encounter in my coaching work that do the same thing. Like everyone else, I am just a human being, and as a human I inherited a few beliefs that served me as a child but no longer served me as an adult.

I find that this "Am I Enough?" syndrome is so prevalent in our society that a few years ago I wrote a children's book for adults that addressed this very issue. It is titled *I Could Love No One Until I Loved Me*. While indirectly it is not a business book, it addresses the impact the formative years and experiences have on our ability to navigate past our fears and discover the lesson that you are enough. It drives home the idea that your self-worth needs to be an inside job and not the responsibility of others around you. (All the proceeds from the book go to help developmentally challenged kids and adults.)

In order to move beyond this point and arrive at a place where we know we are enough, we have to go down through the layers and discard all of the old beliefs and faulty premises that no longer serve us. We have to dig down and weed out all of the beliefs that are giving us the opposite results of what we want.

This process begins with you and ends with you. And once you move forward to discover that you have been placing obstacles in your own path, or refusing to remove the obstacles in your own path be-

CHAPTER 3

cause they give you a certain amount of comfort in a weird kind of way, (or keep you safe and secure), you can begin to remove them. When you learn to clear your path of the obstacles you have put in your path, then and only then, have you earned the privilege to start showing others their path and helping to shine some light on the obstacles that are blocking their path. And that's what leaders do.

CHAPTER 4

FINDING YOUR PATH: START HERE

Places to Start

There are literally hundreds of places to begin the process of self-awareness and you've probably already traveled down a few of these paths over the course of your career. I like to think about it from two possible perspectives. The first path is what we refer to as Outside-In. This is where you go outside of yourself and bring information back in to get insights that will help you see the areas where you might be getting in your own way and in the way of those you lead. It is like being on a boat that has a leak that you cannot find, after you have scoured the boat looking for it. However, sometimes you need to get off the boat and look at it from a different angle so that you can find the leak. And, you find that it was in a place you could only see from an outside perspective or with the help of someone else.

There are two components to this path. One is utilizing assessments and science to give you insights, and the other is to get feedback directly from your leader, peers, direct reports, or others whom you trust. Sometimes our partners and spouses can give us great insight into ourselves if we can get past our egos and pride. Both can be useful as long as they are valid. The validity comes from the intention of the outside factor and sometimes that can be clouded whether it be an organization whose sole purpose is to sell assessments and products,

CHAPTER 4

or a direct report who is simply brown-nosing. It is wise to be cautious when determining the intention as it directly impacts the feedback you will receive.

The second path is what we refer to as Inside-Out and it starts with self-reflection gleaned from repeatedly reliving experiences that we judge as good or bad. For example, if you've been overlooked for a promotion several times, there is a good chance you're not aware of an obstacle in your path, or it may be from soliciting feedback from others in the form of honest and candid conversation with a direct report or peer, or anonymously through a 360-degree assessment.

Outside-In: (Objective Feedback)
Looking Outside to Better Understand the Inside

Outside-In refers to going outside of yourself and utilizing an outside assessment to get in-sight into your behaviors and personailty. It includes Myers-Briggs, DISC, Kolbe, Emergenetics, Predictive Index, Real Colors, Animals—Owl, Peacock, Lion, and the Monkey's Uncle. The most important thing to remember is this: all assessments are not created equal!

While most assessment companies are driven to create revenue, there is a great distinction between an organization that is invested in pushing assessments, and one that is devoted to continuous research and development that strengthens the validity and the depth of the science it supports.

The whole idea of self-awareness is to gain awareness to uncover where you may be getting stuck, and affirm your areas of strength—but more importantly to see how you're impacting others. As a leader you need to be even more aware of how you impact others because these others are reporting directly to you and you have a great deal of influence on them. One of the cornerstones of leadership is your level of Emotional Intelligence (EQ). Research shows that hiring managers are becoming more and more focused on a candidate's EQ versus their

FINDING YOUR PATH: START HERE

IQ, especially when it comes to hiring and promoting leaders. I work with a relatively high percentage of technical leaders who hit a ceiling in their careers because they don't possess the skills they need to lead, coach, and influence people. They rely on their IQ and the technical or tactical side of their brain and ignore the people side of the equation. The best definition I have ever heard when it comes to EQ is from the folks at Target Training International (TTI):

Emotional Intelligence: the ability to sense, understand, and effectively apply the power and acumen of emotions to facilitate higher levels of collaboration and productivity.

One of the most frustrating situations is when I am having a conversation with a leader who refers to EQ as "soft skills." Every time I hear soft skills I cringe.

- Soft—mushy, squashy, slushy, doughy, etc.
- Skills—ability, aptitude, talent, competence, etc.
- Soft skills—a talent for being mushy, slushy, and squashy

When I hear a leader mention the phrase "soft skills" it usually is an indicator that they see a heavy demarcation between the task side of things and the people side of things. They see soft skills and results as mutually exclusive perspectives. They believe that you cannot get results utilizing soft skills and that a harder, more forceful style of leadership is the only way to get results. They don't realize that extraordinary results happen when you influence your team to achieve more than they thought was possible.

A number of years ago, I had a conversation with a CFO who had been on the job less than three weeks at a company. Before he took the time to learn or understand the industry, the history, or the culture of the company, he made the decision to bring in his own people and an outside organization to implement the lean processes that he used at another unrelated company in a completely different industry. Lean technology in and of itself is incredibly valuable. However, if you leave out the people aspect of lean technology, it doesn't sustain. While

CHAPTER 4

explaining himself and his decision, he spouted off words like *kaizen, gemba, gembutsu, kanban, 5S,* and ended the list with um...um...um... uh...oh yeah and "soft skills."

When a leader focuses solely on tasks, process, and dashboards, and forgets the people side of the equation...they fail. When a leader fakes listening to the ideas and input of others knowing that they are going to do what worked at another company regardless of whether or not they understand how the industry or product might be different, they are blinded. When a leader doesn't take the time to understand the perspective of the folks who have been there to understand their challenges, they don't get the buy-in they need to transform the organization. Instead, they replace the employees with their own people who do not understand the industry either, they simply do what worked before. We refer to these leaders as emotionally unintelligent.

Taking assessments is a critical part of leading others because self-management is a core skill needed for Leading, Coaching, & Influencing Others. But taking the assessment is just the beginning of the process. If you don't do anything with the information, and you don't change the way you interact with others, it really doesn't matter, now does it?

The assessment you choose to utilize is critically important. I utilize assessments from the folks at Target Training International. Dr. Ron Bonnstetter is the Senior Vice President of Research and Development and professor emeritus of University of Nebraska in Lincoln. Dr. Bonnstetter drives the research at TTI so that the organization can stay on the cutting edge of brain research and how that research impacts the assessments they provide. Both the validity and reliability scores are high. In fact, they are so accurate that we can use certain assessments and sciences in the selection process without being in violation of the requirements set forth by the Equal Employment Opportunity Commission (EEOC) and The Office of Federal Contract Compliance Programs (OFCCP).

Personal Inventory Bonus: As a gift for purchasing this book, you can have the opportunity to take a Behavioral Assessment to get you started on the path of self-awareness. To get started go to: www.aliveatwork.com/Assessments and click on Leadership Self-Awareness. (You have to enter your name and email so that you can receive your report. Please know we will not call you or sell your name to some Russian Company so they can hack your information. Your information will be kept confidential.)

Outside-In: (Subjective Feedback)
Getting Feedback, Building Trust, & The V-Word

The second aspect of Outside-In, self-awareness, is derived in a more subjective manner. It usually entails direct conversations or indirect surveys from those you interact with at work. This type of feedback doesn't come without challenges; however, the payoff when it is done as part of an overall or ongoing process can be extremely beneficial for you as a leader.

This process can help you gain valuable insight into yourself—not from your perspective—but from the perspective of how your behavior is impacting others. This type of feedback is better than our own assessment of ourselves as we are sometimes blinded by self-perception or ego.

We may have certain beliefs or ideas in our head about who we are and how we interact with others that aren't always accurate or true. Why? Because most people—especially leaders—walk around projecting their beliefs, perceptions, and opinions onto others as if those beliefs, perceptions, and opinions were true for that person. As if we could possibly understand what others see or experience! It is impossible. All we can do is see things from our perspective and our perspective is not the other person's perspective. This concept is a core

CHAPTER 4

principle to grasp if you are going to lead, coach, and influence others. The point here is that in conjunction with an assessment, getting subjective feedback from others is critically important.

The other benefit of asking others for feedback is that it creates opportunities to build relationships by telegraphing the message that you are working to improve yourself. This is a good message to send to your team, especially when you are asking them to do the same.

More importantly, it builds the relationship because you are sending the message that your relationship with them is valuable, valuable enough to work on and invest time in. And, if you value the relationship, you value the person. You don't have to look very far within most organizations to find unhappy employees who do not feel valued. Finally, the very action of asking for feedback about yourself builds trust because it puts you in a vulnerable position and the level of vulnerability is directly correlated to the level of trust between parties.

Trust is a core component that all leaders must establish if they want their people to follow them. Warning: if you think you're leading others and you turn around and no one is behind you, then you're really not leading anyone. Even if you believe that you're trustworthy, it is more important to understand whether or not your people think you are. Trust can always go deeper and wider so maybe you need to take a look...

Some folks also believe that trust is developed over time. While that could be true, it is not an absolute. I know married couples who have been married for 25 years and can't trust each other as far as they can throw each other.

The more vulnerable I am willing to be, the more trust I embody. The hope is that in letting down my guard, the other party will lower their guard, too.

As a leader there are times when trust has to be given before it is earned. This is a matter of trust, and yes you may get burned. You will never know until you try, and it is the responsibility of a leader or a partner in a relationship to decide who to trust and who to be careful around.

48

Before we talk about a process for feedback conversations, I think it is important to realize that if you have been arrogant and walled off for years, you probably shouldn't expect the truth on the first go. Others need to see vulnerability from you first before they will likely open up.

So, how does one go about getting feedback from others? It is actually quite simple!

Here is one possibility of the way a process could look:

1. Schedule an appointment with the person from whom you are seeking feedback. Be very clear and intentional about the purpose (the *why* as well as the *what* you are hoping to gain from the conversation). This needs to happen up-front so they are not caught off guard, wondering, or trying to figure out how to prepare for the conversation.

   "I was wondering if we could schedule some time for a conversation. I am in the process of understanding how my leadership is impacting others and I need your help. I need about 15 minutes of your time..."

2. When you begin the conversation it is important that you do not ask questions that would lead or guide them to give you the feedback that you want to steer them toward. If this occurs, you will be getting data that is tainted because they are trying to read your mind. This process could be uncomfortable for some, especially direct reports who may be afraid to give you direct feedback or feedback that isn't so wonderful. The more general the questions the better. Once you ask a question, do not add any more words or descriptions, especially if they're not responding as quickly as you like and you are getting uncomfortable with the silence.

   a. "What is it that I do as a leader that really works for you?"

   b. "What is it that doesn't work for you?"

   c. "If there was just one thing I could do as your leader that would be most helpful to you, what would it be?" If you get a vague answer or it is something that is hard to see, measure, or do, ask them the following question: "What would that look like to you if I was doing more x or y or z? How often?" (We will get farther into this later, but for now this should serve you very well.)

3. Last question: "Is there more? Is there anything else?"
4. "Thank you for the feedback, it is greatly appreciated!"
5. You are done...for now.

I said for now, because if you don't do anything with the information, if you go back to your old ways after a week or two, you will inevitably do more damage than good. Why? Because you are sending that person the message that you do not do what you say you are going to do when you say you are going to do it. In other words, you can't be trusted and we all know where that realization will take you as a leader. Just like assessments, if you don't do anything with it, if you don't take actions, you are wasting not just your time and theirs ...you are damaging your brand as a leader.

Inside-Out

The value of self-awareness from the Inside-Out is that it usually is real and not imagined. If your lack of self-awareness has gotten to a point where it is causing stress and problems for you and the folks you interact with, it may be time for some real down-to-earth soul-searching.

Self-reflection is the ability to look inside the self in order to see where the strengths are, as well as areas for development (otherwise known as weaknesses) and where these are impacting the ability to lead others. Let's face it, some folks are more self-aware than others. The question becomes: How do you know if you have a low level of self-awareness from the inside out?

Here are a few possibilities:

3 Signs You Have Low Inside-Out Level of Self-Awareness:

1. You've heard subtle hints or straightforward between-the-eyes feedback from your boss, peers, or partner that you have issues, and it has resulted in you being passed over for a promotion more times than an 80-year-old driving his Buick on an L.A. freeway at rush hour, yet you still believe...you're fine...or it's not you or your problem? Guess what? It's your problem! Chances are you have little to no self-awareness and are in denial about yourself as a leader. Sometimes we human beings need pain to wake up! If the first part of this is true for you and yet you are applying for every single in-house promotion and have been turned down by all of them —and, although the interviewers tell you you're a great candidate, but they went with someone else who was a better fit 20 times in a row, you may have a low level of self-awareness. Better to ask yourself: *What am I doing that is creating this situation?* This is not a time to blame your boss, the interviewer, or the fact that you didn't make the cut for the high-school football team. However, it may be a good time to go outside of yourself for feedback from others.

2. You find that you have lost your desire to lead others, or you never really had it but you like the title and the money. This can be caused by your inability to be successful as a leader, not getting results, being burned out, or just plain boredom. I always have felt that if a leader is not loving their job and is not succeeding at their job, it is due to one of three reasons:

    a. They do not have the skills to do the job and so they need to be: **Coached and Trained**.

    b. They are not a good fit for a leadership position or they just don't have the desire to do what it takes to be a leader; however, they are a great employee. Sometimes people like the idea of being a leader more than then they like actually being a leader. If they really don't want to

CHAPTER 4

be a leader: **Move over and make room for someone who does**.

c. They have a bad attitude, a leadership entitlement mentality, or they are lazy and have a work ethic issue and so it's appropriate to **Coach them** until a shift or change occurs. And if a shift doesn't happen—**move them out**.

This applies to leadership as much as it applies to those folks who report directly to you. Most leaders prolong these decisions and hope the situation will turn itself around by itself. It never does.

3. If your personal life and health are suffering in any way, it could be any of the following:

Mental—Constant headaches or feeling stressed.

Emotional—You are always angry or unhappy and a bear to be around.

Spiritual—I don't mean religiously, I mean if you have a constant disturbance in your inner self and it doesn't go away.

Physical—Physical symptoms such as headaches, back pain, intestinal and digestive issues. These can be simply reflections of an inner turmoil or dis-ease telling you that you are not in alignment with who you are and how you want your life to be.

Sure you can push back against these issues, and I have seen folks so out of alignment with who they are and what they want that it literally made them ill. The impact that stress has on depleting your immune system is staggering and scientifically factual.

If any of these symptoms are showing up in your life, you might need a serious wake up call!

If this is the case, you need to come to grips with the facts of your reality, own it, and take action to course correct. As I see it, here are your choices:

52

1. You can get help by hiring a coach, a therapist, or investing in yourself to get the training you need to be a better leader.
2. You can walk away from being a leader because it isn't what you truly want or desire.
3. You need to find a position that better suits you, whether it is in the company for which you are currently employed, or someplace else.

Just remember: Wherever you go, there you are!

Practicing the Art
What's your AQ (Awareness Quotient)?

Once you have reviewed your Leadership Self-Awareness Assessment results that you took at www.aliveatwork.com/Assessments, ask yourself the following questions:
1. What did I learn about myself and my value to the organization that surprised me?
2. In the Areas for Improvement section of the assessment, what is the area that keeps coming up in my feedback from others or in other assessments I have taken?
3. What could I do to improve in this area so that I can increase my effectiveness as a leader?

CHAPTER 5
ARE YOU A LEADER OR A GLORIFIED INDIVIDUAL CONTRIBUTOR?

In Chapter 1 we defined a leader as *someone who influences others to do or to be their best*. But, different leaders have different ideas about what that actually entails. At one time or another we have all worked for a leader who was all about being in control, but they couldn't step back from the actual work. In a sense, this type of leader is acting in the capacity of an individual contributor (IC) instead of a leader.

I was working with a client who was a director-level leader at a very large investment bank. She shared numerous stories about her leader, who was constantly in the weeds. One of her stories was about her leader adjusting the margins of her reports in the report documents. According to her boss, the Vice President, he wanted the margins a certain way. Margins…really?

It's one thing if you want it a certain way because you're anal retentive and/or a control freak, at least own your faults instead of making excuses to cover up your obsessive compulsive disorder by blaming it on someone else. I am not saying it's okay, but at least be honest with yourself and own your issue. If the Vice President feels the need to be that far into the weeds, it is a sign that there is a leadership vacuum within the culture, and leaders are just acting in the capacity of a glorified individual contributor (GIC) and not truly leading.

CHAPTER 5

The Biggest Jump You Will Ever Make

It has been well-documented that the single most difficult jump a leader must make is the jump from being an individual contributor to a leader of people. Why? Because the skills that got you promoted from an individual contributor to a leader are not the skills that will ensure your success as a leader. Being a leader was never going to be easy. In fact, I believe that being a genuine leader is one of the greatest challenges that you will face in your career.

One of the first ideas you need to embrace is the fundamental shift in how you perceive your work and how you go about getting things done. As an individual contributor (IC) you were directly responsible for making things happen. When something needed to get done, you did it! And you did it *your* way and in *your* time frame; for the most part you were in control. When you become a leader your job requires that you step back from the IC role and influence others to get the work done. As you move up in position, you have to continue to step back farther and farther from the actual work and influence at a higher and higher level.

The problem is that you find out that most people don't do things the exact same way you do, or with the same level of urgency. You find out that some people let their personal lives get in the way of their work, and still others don't have the confidence or want the responsibility to step up and put their neck on the line for fear of making a mistake or being reprimanded.

What becomes so frustrating is that for the life of you, you can't understand why people won't or don't see things the same way you do. After a while, your frustration builds and either you start trying to micromanage your team's behaviors, or you throw your hands up, jump in, and do the work yourself, because it's easier and faster. After all, it was your ability to get results that got you promoted in the first place. This is how a leader can get dragged in the between-worlds of quasi-contributor and quasi-leader, doing neither of those positions

56

effectively. Some leaders stay stuck in this land between worlds their entire careers and never get to the point of effectively leading others. It's like the Catholic version of purgatory, except for leaders.

Why Most Leaders Fail

You can see that whether you've been leading for 6 weeks, 6 months, or more than 6 years, you may be just acting like a GIC. Here are some of the problems that happen if and when you get stuck here:

Problem #1: Your talent will leave — If you have 10 or 20 people reporting, you may be able to micromanage for a period of time. But eventually your really good people, the talented ones and the millennials, realize that they are not challenged, don't feel valued or trusted, and more importantly they don't feel like they have any control over how their job is done. So they decide to find employment somewhere else, whether it is another department in the company, or your competitor at another company!

Problem #2: You don't scale — As the size of your organization grows, you find that attempting to micromanage 50 people is much more difficult than micromanaging 20 of them, and the idea of attempting to micromanage 200 folks seems like pure insanity. In other words, you don't scale, because your leadership style doesn't work with large numbers of people. Yes, it is true you will have managers underneath you to manage those folks. However, if you have people underneath you who are strong leaders and who don't like to be micromanaged, then Problem #1 will occur and they will leave as well. This might be a good time to remind you of the old adage that people leave bosses and managers, they rarely leave companies or extraordinary leaders. Extraordinary results happen when your entire team is producing at their highest levels.

CHAPTER 5

Problem #3: You lead from a place of force — The inability to make the jump from GIC to being a leader probably means that you are leading from a place of force instead of a place of power (refer back to Chapter 2). People do not like to be controlled. They don't like being told what to do. When your leadership is self-centered, your team knows that you don't have their back and so they don't have yours. Leading from a position of force sends all the wrong messages to your team about their value and their worth, and it robs them of having a sense of purpose or doing meaningful work. Eventually they get tired of it and move on. If they complain enough to the right people, you may end up being the person who moves on.

The need to control others by micromanaging is rooted in fear. Fear of losing control, looking bad, not being right, being seen in a poor light, or losing in some way. It gets worse...

Your Worst Nightmare

Leading is about bringing out the best in others, it is not about telling others what to do or how to do it. The real issue here is that what normally happens when we are exhibiting behaviors out of a place of fear is that we end up realizing or experiencing the very thing we fear most: our worst nightmare.

I once worked with a moderately-sized family business. It was run by two very successful businessmen who had taken the company far beyond where they ever thought it would or could go. Both of these men each had a son in the business. Their biggest fear was that as they got older their sons would be unable to take over the business, and everything they had worked for would be driven into the ground. The owners kept such tight control on the kids that they never really let them take the lead on anything. Folks in the industry held the same fear, that when the two owners retired, nobody would be able to step in and lead the organization into the future. I'm sure it impacted some of their decisions to expand with them at times.

One day we were having a conversation and I said to the owners in so many words: Watching you two lead the company is like watching a pilot and a co-pilot fly a plane. Sitting behind you in first class are your kids who keep peering into the cockpit and wondering what it would be like to fly the plane and hold the controls. However, you never really invite them up front for long enough, so they are missing out on the opportunity to learn how to fly the plane through some of the turbulence and storms that happen in the normal course of flying. One day both of you are going to die and your kids are going to have to come up to the cockpit and fly the plane. The only problem is that they never got enough hours and experience in the cockpit because you wouldn't let go of the controls. So what do you think is going to happen when the first big storm hits? They're going to drive it into the ground! Isn't that your worst nightmare? I finished by reminding them that their role as leaders is not to tell them what to do or how to do it. It is to teach them how you think! (More about this in Chapter 8.)

At some point, you have to let go and trust your team to get the work done. You can't do that if you are acting like an IC and controlling everything. People sense when you trust them and when you don't. And, if you don't trust them, why should they trust you? Remember: People don't follow leaders they don't trust!

Where Do You Stand?

How do you know if you're playing on the leader side of the equation or if you're still rooting around in the IC role?

10 Statements to Help You Determine If You're a Leader or a Glorified Individual Contributor:
(**Answer true or false**)

1. When I get frustrated with the progress others are making, I step in by having accountability conversations with my team members to get them back on track.

CHAPTER 5

2. I consistently begin conversations with general questions on a topic to first understand what the other person is thinking.

3. I honestly believe that helping others get their needs met first increases the probability of me getting my needs met faster than if I was to focus on meeting my needs first.

4. I give honest feedback on a consistent basis to my team members so they know how they are performing. Performance issue conversations are never a surprise.

5. I know that my role as a leader is to influence others to do or to be their best, whether I have direct reports or not.

6. When I am in emotionally stressful situations, I have the ability to separate the event that is happening from the emotional way I respond to it.

7. I consistently invest in my development and have attended a seminar or read a leadership book in the last 45 days.

8. I am happy at least 75% of the time since I took the leadership position, and I have no regrets about doing so.

9. I am effective in my ability to influence others in 1-on-1 situations (coaching), 1-on-10 situations (facilitating), and 1-on-100 situations (presentations).

10. I took the leadership position because I know that I was called to be a leader—not only because of the money, status, or title.

Scoring: Add up how many times you answered true to each statement.

- **If you scored 8 or more**—Congratulations! You are well on your way to being an effective leader and are much less of an IC!

- **If you scored a 6 or 7**—You need to make a few changes to your approach to leadership. Look at the statements in which you answered "false" and ask yourself what would you need to do to make that statement true.

- **If you scored 5 or less**—You probably need to take a good look at how you're leading. Obviously the lower the score, the less effective you are as a leader. It may be time to reevaluate what

ARE YOU A LEADER OR A GLORIFIED INDIVIDUAL CONTRIBUTOR?

you truly want out of your work. Remember, it is perfectly okay to step back and be an IC. You may find that you are much happier and more effective as an IC then you could ever be as a leader. If you decide you want to down the leadership path, you may want to revisit statement 7 above, and take action today.

CHAPTER 6
LEADING AUTHENTICALLY

P eople throw words around without much thought. Turn on the television and it seems as if authenticity is the word of the day. The word *authenticity* has been inserted into dialogues and interviews from Oprah to Anderson Cooper. From popes to presidential candidates, all have spoken about the importance of being authentic. It seems like it has become a generic word, like "Kleenex®" and that at times, the lines between meanings and definitions blur and words such as integrity, authenticity, honesty, genuine, and truth all seem to blend together so that they are used interchangeably. When this happens, none of these words holds much meaning or value.

Authenticity is a result of people being honest and telling the truth. Most people believe that politicians are inauthentic because they don't tell the truth and they are dishonest. Watching an interview of a politician, you see them carefully selecting their words in order to shape their message. When a politician uses profanity, it is considered politically incorrect, therefore most will not use profanity, and look down on their colleagues that do. However, an article published in *Social Psychology and Personality Science* shows that the use of profanity is associated with genuine feelings—yes genuine or authentic feelings. So, who is being authentic? The politically correct politician or the one who cusses like a sailor because nothing is getting done? Authenticity can be a confusing and complicated topic. Or is it?

I am a firm believer in simplicity, especially when it comes to the truth. There are times during coaching sessions when I ask someone a simple yes or no question and in response receive a dissertation back in the form of a long drawn-out story. When this happens I usually get the sense that they are trying to convince me that they did the right thing, are thinking the right way, or are justifying their thought process or position. Sometimes I believe they are trying to convince themselves that what they are saying is correct.

I am reminded of this again when I am watching the news and a politician is asked a simple question but doesn't provide a straightforward answer in return. Their response has nothing to do with the question and everything to do with their agenda, which is to mask the truth, or shape your perception of the topic in a way that isn't quite true.

Being a leader who influences others well means you have to be authentic with yourself before you can be authentic with others.

The Relationship Between Integrity & Authenticity

Years ago when I was married, my wife and I were going through a rough patch and so we separated for a while. After a short time, we reconciled and in celebration of our decision, we threw a party. At that point my life was pretty compartmentalized because I felt the need to keep all my facades (faces) very far apart. My church friends were separate from my work colleagues, who were separate from my in-laws, who were...you get the picture. I'll never forget walking outside onto the patio at our get-back-together celebration with a pitcher of margaritas while I was hearing bits and snippets of all the conversations that were taking place.

To my right was my dear elderly friend, Helen, whom I met when she first read my tarot cards. She was smoking a cigarette and deeply engaged in a conversation with Susan, a very conservative Christian woman from my church, who was married to my friend Steve. I can still see the word bubbles over their heads. "Susan: So how did you meet Joe?" Helen, in her raspy, throaty, smoker's voice: "Well, if you must know the truth, I read his ta-roooooooo carrrrrrrrrrrrrrs." The words just hung there in slow motion over their heads as if time and space had grinded to a screeching halt.

Like George Costanza in a bad Seinfeld episode, my worlds were colliding, my life was blowing up, they were killing independent Joe!

I turned to the left where my friend, Phil, from my men's group, was explaining a little bit about our group retreats to my brother-in-law Bruce, my wife's older, overly protective brother who never really liked me. Did I mention both he and his brother were cops? I swear I heard Phil finishing his sentence with "...running naked through the woods!" Of course I'm sure that wasn't what was being spoken...it's just what I heard!

The walls that I had constructed to keep me safe and separate were crumbling all around me. I was exposed! The truth is I was out of integrity. Why? Because my life wasn't integrated. I felt like I had to be a different person in each and every group.

When it comes to integrity as a leader it's important to be able to ask yourself: Am I the same person with my team in the office as I am with them at happy hour? Am I the same person at happy hour on Friday night with my friends as I am at church on Sunday morning with my family?

Sure, I understand the need to adjust your behaviors in different situations. However, I am talking about who you are at your core.

The more you separate yourself, the more out of integrity you are because the pieces and parts of your life are not connected and whole. Keeping up facades and living separate lives will eventually rear its ugly head, it is just a matter of time. You might be thinking that this is an extreme example, and yet we are in shock watching the nightly news after some tragedy unfolded and the reporter is interviewing the neighbors and coworkers, "He was always a quiet person and a great neighbor, I'm shocked." Or more subtly and closer to home, "I'm shocked, they were together for 25 years and always seemed like they were so happy together, I can't believe they're getting a divorce."

The point here is if you have to play all these different roles at different times with different people, how can you be authentic? Besides, which one of those facades is the real you?

At some point your true self will come out because trying to hold all these masks and facades up is like trying to hold a beach ball under water in the pool. Eventually you are going to get tired and that thing is going to launch out from under you like a rocket while you sink like an anchor.

People are pretty good judges of character—especially when they are in a position that requires trust. They know when they're getting manipulated no matter how eloquently you speak or what you say. Think Bill Clinton, "It depends on what the definition of is...is?"

To put it simply, you are either being truthful or you're not, period, the end.

Let me let you in on a little secret. As a leader, you cannot give away something you do not have, so if you demand honesty and integrity from your people but you don't have it yourself, you're out of integrity and it doesn't work.

There are Universal Laws that apply to this world (laws that cannot be broken) and The Law of Reciprocity is one of them. If you want something in return, you first have to be willing to give it.

For example, if you want honesty from others, you have to be honest with them first. If you want respect from your people, you have to be willing to give them respect first.

If you find your life compartmentalized and feel that you need to be someone else, especially as a leader, now might be a good time to ask yourself the question: What makes you feel like you can't be who you are? Or, What do you believe is so wrong with you that you feel like who you are isn't enough?

Being Who You Are

Chapter 3 discussed the topic of being enough, and I shared with you the idea that many people walk around trying to prove they are enough to themselves, their peers, and even their parents. When it comes to authenticity, there are those who feel that if people really knew who was underneath the facade, they would run away. And so the true self is kept buried behind the many facades that show up in the workplace:

- Einstein — I am the smartest person in the room (this can be spoken or unspoken, aggressive, passive aggressive or passive).
- Mr./Mrs. Never Enough — I will prove my worth to you by over-achieving and standing out.
- The Congressman — I declare with my words that it is all about my team but it's really all about me.
- The Impostor — I am the sweet, caring, and considerate boss when all of us are in front of the V.P., but in our meetings I will ride your behind like Seattle Slew at the Kentucky Derby and drive you into the ground because of my own inadequacies.
- Do You See Me — I will talk louder and say things I don't normally say when I am on the phone and others can hear me.
- The Procrastinator — I am so busy I don't have enough time to do my work, but I have enough time to stand here and tell you I don't have enough time to do my work.

Yes, we all know these facades and I am sure you have a few of your own that come to mind. It would be easy to judge these people as bad or look to the core of what drives people to put on a facade and say: "Wow, it must really suck to have to show up and try to be someone you're not because you don't believe you're enough." I'm not asking you to play therapist. I'm simply saying a little empathy might go a

CHAPTER 6

long way, especially as a leader, when you see these behaviors going on in your department with your team.

My coaching clients are really good people who just need a little more self-awareness. They are not broken, they are not fatally flawed, they are great people who place obstacles in their own path, and these obstacles prevent them from moving forward to get where they want to go and live the lives they want to live.

You are no different. As a coach, you need to help your team members see and then remove their own obstacles, and that makes you a more effective leader. But remember: You can't help others remove their obstacles if you keep supplanting land mines in front of you on your path to success.

Trusting Who You Are

Self-awareness is a great tool to help you learn more about how you behave, why you behave in a particular way, and even your level of Emotional Intelligence (EQ).

However, if the underlying belief is that you're not good enough or that you have to be someone other than who you truly are in order to gain acceptance, all of the assessments and self-awareness will not make you a great leader.

If you've ever seen the *Wizard of Oz,* you know that toward the end of the movie when Dorothy's dog Toto pulls back the curtain to expose the almighty and powerful Wizard of Oz as a phony, you will understand this idea of facades. The wizard thought he had to be somebody else. He didn't trust that he could be his authentic self, or that he was good enough, so he conjured up a giant facade to appear more powerful and all-knowing. He didn't trust or believe in himself, so he put on a mask and pretended to be someone else. At one point after Dorothy discovers the truth, she says to him: "You're a very bad man!" And he replies, "Oh no, my dear, I'm a very good man, I'm just a very bad wizard!" It wasn't until he owned the truth of who he was,

68

and trusted who he was, that he could actually help Dorothy and her friends to achieve what they had set out to do.

You are creative, resourceful, and whole. You may have been imprinted with beliefs that told you who you are wasn't good enough. You may have had some experiences along the way in which you got burned and so you promised yourself never to stick your neck out because it might get chopped off—again.

Part of evolving as a human being and as a leader means that at times you have to look at some of the beliefs you hold, and shift them or even get rid of them. This is especially true for those beliefs that may be holding you back, or those beliefs that are giving you the opposite results of what you want.

As a leader, it is important to leverage the talents and brilliance of your team members in the areas that are not your strengths. Being able to recognize what you don't do very well is as important as knowing what it is that you do. In the end, rediscovering your authentic self and living from a place of integrity is really about rediscovering who you truly are. It's about being clear about your strengths, your genius, and your brilliance, and then living and leading from them. When you operate from a place of authenticity and integrity, you are providing your maximum value to others.

CHAPTER 7
LEADING FROM YOUR STRENGTHS

L eading from your strengths for some leaders is an oxymoron. Meaning, most leaders don't focus on strengths, they spend extraordinary amounts of time focusing on their own weaknesses and the weaknesses of their team members. And, while learning and improving is a critical part of developing yourself and others, some never move beyond the constant attention to the things they don't do well. Strong leaders, however, focus on and embrace all of the things they do incredibly well.

Uncovering Your Strengths

There is an immense amount of research, particularly from the Gallup organization, on the benefits of focusing on people's strengths. It has been my experience, both personally and in working with hundreds and hundreds of clients, that when you're working and leading from your strengths, it doesn't feel like work. When your strengths are aligned with the requirements of the job, you unleash the maximum value and impact on your organization, your team, and the world around you. The result: Your job is much easier and you are much happier because you are doing what comes naturally to you.

CHAPTER 7

The reverse is also true. When your strengths are not aligned with your job, when you're struggling because who you are and your natural strengths are not aligned with what is required 8-12 hours a day, it can cause a tremendous amount of stress. When this happens you have two options: Either you can shift your perspective on how you are viewing your work and look for ways to align yourself with your work, or you can change jobs. Most people gravitate to changing jobs before they have clarity on their strengths because while they may intrinsically know what they do well, they don't have a tool or assessment that gives them the insight needed to identify those strengths in a succinct and concise manner. That is why the very first step in this process is to discover or rediscover your strengths.

Here's where to begin:

I have searched for years to find an assessment or process to help my clients uncover their strengths, and the best tool I have found is the StrengthsFinder® Assessment from Gallup. You can purchase the assessment directly online or you can access the assessment through a code embedded in each StrengthsFinder 2.0 book. There are a few different versions and it is available in a variety of languages. The book will provide you with an opportunity to learn more about yourself and others whose strengths might be different than yours. The book also goes into much more depth. As a leader, I think this information can be extremely helpful. I do not receive any type of compensation for recommending this tool, I simply believe that it is the best resource out there for you.

Leading From Your Strengths

If you choose to take the assessment, once you receive your results you will see a ranking for all thirty-four of your strengths beginning with top five. The area to focus on for the purpose of this exercise is not all thirty-four, but only the top five. Gallup would refer to these as your "DNA" and I believe it is where you should spend the majority of your time and focus. For some, the results will be crystal clear and you will feel affirmed in your results. Some of you may have further questions, and so I highly recommend you read up on each strength that you find in the book or online so that you understand how Gallup defines them. This is critically important because you may place a different meaning on the word, activator, or connectedness and it might cause you to misinterpret your results.

Once you have your top five strengths and you understand them, write them down in a column on a sheet of paper and then rank them on a scale of 1 to 10 (1 being low and 10 being high) and answer the following question for each strength:

How well am I utilizing my _____ strength in my work as a leader?
Once you have the strengths ranked, you may discover that you have one of three realizations:

1. You are completely leveraging your strengths as a leader on a consistent basis.
2. You are not fully leveraging all of your strengths to their fullest impact and, therefore, you need to determine how you can bring more of the strengths that you are not engaging into your daily work.
3. You aren't awake and conscious of your strengths. You are not utilizing them in your work as a leader and you need to shift your approach by embracing this new information.

If you are one of the fortunate people in category one, congratulations! If not, that's okay, whether you have a few areas to work on, or you are just uncovering your strengths for the first time, you have an incredible opportunity for growth.

CHAPTER 7

Embracing Your Strength Will Get You Engaged and...

You now have a list of your top five strengths and you have rated them on a scale of 1 to 10. Take the strength you rated the lowest and ask yourself the following questions:

1. What would it look like if I was fully utilizing my _____ strength?
2. What is it costing me (relationally, satisfactorily, related to empowerment) to not engage this strength in my leadership and in my work?
3. How could I engage this strength more effectively in my work?
4. What is one action I could take for the next 10 days to engage this strength even more (Ask yourself if the action is definable, measurable, and actionable. You should be able to answer yes or no to each question.)
5. To whom will I be accountable so that I can honor my commitment to myself?
6. How will I know if it is working?

And when you do this, here is what you will find: You will find that engaging your strengths is extremely fulfilling, and that it is much easier to be engaged when you are working from your strengths than it is when you are beating yourself up for your weaknesses.

You may need to shift your perspective and how you are viewing your work so that you see it through the lens of your strengths. It is important to understand that you need to do this in the context of being a leader and not an individual contributor. This is critically important because it may reveal that you have been approaching your job as a leader more like an individual contributor and need to transition into the leadership role. Part of doing self-reflective exercises is to see how beliefs are out of alignment with the results we truly want. The human mind is quite capable of rationalizing so that it sees what it wants to see and not what is needed in order to move forward in growth and development.

74

It is possible that after this exercise you come to the realization your work and your most authentic self is not a fit. This actually happens more often than you may think because many times we put bodies in positions instead of making sure the person is a fit for the position. Many times when someone leaves an organization unexpectedly, the job responsibilities are divvied up in order to absorb the work. Or, we are in such a hurry to fill a position as the organization expands that we step over the due diligence of understanding the reason the job exists, the job requirements, and whether those align with the strengths of the person we are considering.

Regardless of your conclusion, it requires that you take action. Whether it is to move forward and improve what you are already doing, embrace your strengths at an even higher level, or find a position that that truly aligns with who you are and what you want, you need to take action. Make a decision and act on it. The damage that you do to yourself and others by staying in a position that lacks purpose and meaning, or that doesn't leverage your strengths, will take you farther and farther off your path and away from your purpose.

Finding Your Path...Leading Others to Theirs

If you do the work to discover your strengths and embrace those strengths, you will find that your work doesn't feel like work and it will become much easier for you. When you love what you do and you're good at it, people will notice. And when you consistently get noticed for what you do well, you will know you are on the path toward your purpose. At first you may think that other people have the same strengths as you, or you may downplay your strengths because they come so naturally to you and it is easy. However, that isn't the case. Each individual has a unique blend of strengths that make them who they are. Once you discover your strengths and embrace them, you are now able to lead others by helping them discover their strengths and their path as well.

CHAPTER 7

In his book *Aspire,* Kevin Hall breaks down the meaning of the word leader. *Lea* means path, and *der* means to find. A leader, therefore, is a pathfinder. This is someone with a vision who can see the big picture, and who helps others to discover their path.

However, you cannot help others find their path if you are not on your own path. You cannot give away something you don't have; it's an integrity issue.

After you have gone through this process of identifying your strengths, and becoming more intentional about leading from them, then I challenge you to pay it forward.

Take your team members through the same process, help them to uncover their strengths and work from them. Why? Because that is what leaders are, they are pathfinders, and they help others to reach their highest potential. Helping people discover their strengths is just one of the ways to lead people to become the best version of themselves they can be.

CHAPTER 8
CREATING YOUR LEADERSHIP STRATEGY

U p until this point, we have defined leadership, influence, and what it looks like to be a leader who influences others. We have talked about the differences between leading from a place of Power versus a place of Force, and that you are completely responsible for the impact you make (or don't make) as a leader.

We have provided tools and resources for you to increase your level of self-awareness so that you can leverage your talents and strengths, and we have shared the importance of being your authentic self as a leader.

Now it is time to take all of this information and develop your strategy, your plan, and the actions you will need to take to help you reach your highest leadership potential. Hopefully, you now have more than enough insight into why you chose to be a leader, your strengths, and the areas that will require attention. Most importantly, I hope you now know more clearly than ever before why you decided to become a leader. Remember, without the why, the how and the what don't matter. If you are unclear about why you became a leader, the rest of the book that delves into the hows and whats of Coaching and Influencing will be worthless. In fact, if you are still unclear why you became a leader, I suggest that you put this book down and re-evaluate your position because you can't be an extraordinary leader if

CHAPTER 8

you don't know *why* you became a leader. You might be able to manage processes or tasks, but you will never truly lead people.

This chapter is all about action, change, and your willingness to be a more influential leader.

Don't Be a Floyd

A number of years ago I was leading a Leadership Development Program for a team of leaders. The team had a wide range of leadership experiences ranging anywhere from three weeks to twenty years.

One of the gentlemen came in knowing a lot. In fact, he knew everything because he had been in "so many of these leadership classes, they're pretty much all the same." At the moment he voiced those words a thought occurred to me, and I asked him this question: "If you have been to so many of these trainings, why do your managers feel the need to keep sending you?"

Like Floyd, many of you have attended numerous trainings and have probably read a diatribe of leadership books. If not, I am grateful that you chose the book that is currently in your hands.

The rule is that you forget 75% of what you learn when you walk out the door after a training program. If you don't utilize the concepts or ideas within thirty days, the retention rate drops by 95%, meaning that you will have only retained 5% of what you initially learned. Whether you learn and grow is based on the relationship between repetition and retention. In other words, the more you use it, the less you lose it.

When you consider the cost of training after you add up time, money, lost production, and any additional resources, a less than 5% retention rate is quite dismal and that would indicate that your return-on-investment is practically nonexistent. Whether you walked out of the class with one or one hundred great ideas, if you don't implement them on a consistent basis, it was a waste of time.

78

Sustaining Long-Lasting Change

Knowledge without action is meaningless unless you just like to talk a lot. One of the problems with going to a lot of seminars and workshops is that you get so many ideas and you create multiple to-do lists and rarely put anything into place long enough to experience long-lasting change. Recall that your beliefs drive your behaviors (actions) and your actions produce the results you are getting in your life. Further, the results you get in life just reaffirm your beliefs. (See the model below.)

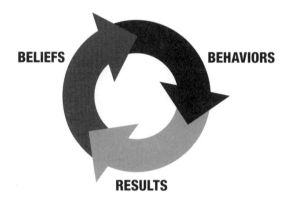

Re-Beliefing Process

If your belief about money is that it is scarce and there is never enough, because that is the way you grew up, then no matter how much you make there will never be enough because your underlying belief drives your actions.

You will probably never be happy in this area of your life because you will constantly strive for more. Why? Because in your mind you will never have enough. This is one driving force behind greed: the incessant feeling that you need more. The insanity of this is that your results simply reaffirm the belief and you get stuck in a never-ending cycle. It becomes a self-fulfilling prophecy.

CHAPTER 8

If you believe you are a lousy leader, then everything you see will be through the lens of a lousy leader. Then, you will look for opportunities to prove that you are correct. You may even do things that sabotage your career or your relationships because you are heavily invested in the belief that you are a lousy leader. It serves you in some unhealthy way and thus becomes a self-fulfilling prophecy.

In order to effect long-lasting change, you cannot simply change your behaviors because behaviors will always find congruence and re-align with your beliefs. You may change for a short time, but before you know it, your behaviors will go back into alignment with your beliefs.

Think about the meetings at work where everyone agrees to change their behaviors, and as a group you list all of the things to start doing as well as the things you need to stop doing as a group. Three weeks later you and your team are having another meeting about the very same topic because the group never got aligned with the underlying belief needed to sustain long-lasting change. If you say "we will hold each other accountable" but team members around the table all have different ideas about what accountability means, then you've wasted your time...again.

Re-Beliefing Your Beliefs

A number of years ago I was doing a workshop for a sales team, and like a lot of salespeople, they despised the idea of making cold calls and prospecting for new business with potential customers they didn't know or had never met—even though every salesperson knows that prospecting and getting new clients is the key to sustaining a business. We were discussing this concept of re-beliefing what they were making prospecting mean, and the underlying beliefs that they were attaching to the topic. I heard words such as abhor, despise, hard, difficult, and rejection.

I asked the folks to raise their hands if they liked having conversations with people, and they all emphatically raised their hands. Of course

80

CREATING YOUR LEADERSHIP STRATEGY

they do, they are salespeople and most salespeople talk too much. I then said, "So what if you reframed the whole idea of prospecting and made prospecting mean this?": *Prospecting is having conversations with people to see if the possibility of doing business together might exist.*

It was a complete and total shift and it worked. Nearly every salesperson in that group achieved their target to acquire new business that year.

So what does this have to do with you?

Everything!

Pull out a piece of paper and draw a line down the center of the page.

In the left hand column, at the top of the page, write down the word "Beliefs." Then, write down what you believe, truly believe when no one is around, about being a leader. Second, write down what you believe about conflict. Third, write down what you believe about delegation. You can do this with communication, marriage, accountability, conflict, or other topics, but for now just stick to the leadership topic.

Next, in the column on the right, on a scale of 1 to 10 with 10 being extremely high and 1 being extremely low, rate yourself on the results you are getting in those areas you wrote on the left side of the page (leadership, conflict resolution, and delegation). If you've done the exercise properly, your belief will align with your results and vice-versa. The question you have to ask yourself is: Are you getting the results you truly want as a leader? If not, you may have to examine the underlying belief and reframe it so that it aligns with the results you really want.

I worked with a Managing Director for a Fortune 50 company who shared his underlying belief with me about being a leader. He said: "Joe, I love the corner office, I love the pay and the title, if I just didn't have to deal with all the people stuff, I would have the perfect job!"

My thought: And you wonder why you're having challenges and none of your people trust or respect you? Hmmmm I'm stuck...let me think about this one!!

What old beliefs are you holding on to that may be holding you back from being a more effective leader?

81

What past experiences (or leaders that you have worked for) shaped how you see your role as a leader?

Is there a belief you are holding onto about your style, personality, years as a leader, education or lack of, that is creating an obstacle in front of you?

To complete the process, ask yourself what results you are trying to achieve. For example:

If you want to be more influential as a leader, your underlying beliefs could be:
- I consistently listen to understand the situation or problem before jumping to conclusions or giving my opinion.

If you avoid having the difficult conversations with your people:
- I address performance issues and have the uncomfortable conversations as quickly as possible.

If you struggle with delegation:
- I set clear expectations when making requests of others and then let others decide how to accomplish those tasks.

If you struggle with needing to tell people how to do things:
- I ask great questions so that my folks can find solutions to their challenges and problems.

If you struggle with holding others accountable:
- I meet regularly with my employees to check in with them on the commitments they made in our one-on-one meetings.

It is important that you don't over commit here, and make sure that what you are committing to moves you beyond your comfort zone. Start small and work on one specific belief for at least ten days. There will be times when it doesn't go so well and you have to give yourself a little grace and compassion. This is a process and you won't perfect it in one day.

CREATING YOUR LEADERSHIP STRATEGY

The Cost of Not Changing?

Most people don't decide to change because they are doing marvelously. Most people change when there is a great deal of pain or loss involved in their situation. In his book *Change or Die,* Alan Deutschman shared the following statistics:

- The healthcare industry consumes $2.1 trillion dollars each year.
- More than 1.5 million people undergo coronary bypass surgery or angioplasty at a total price of about $60 billion dollars.
- Fewer than 3% of the surgical procedures performed prevented heart attacks or prolonged their lives.
- Two years after coronary artery bypass grafting 9% of the patients had not changed the lifestyle that was adding to or creating their issues.

When a person's life is on the line and it is a matter of life or death people still did not change.

Can you see why getting people to make a few changes in how they lead and influence others might be futile? Looking at the cost of not changing may help you to decide what you truly want as a leader.

This is why it is critically important that you understand why you want to be a leader in the first place. This is why you have to embrace the concept that being a leader is not a reward for performance or an entitlement; it is a privilege and it is a calling.

A mentor of mine once asked me if I was interested in seeking success or if I wanted to experience significance. At the time, I had been going 120 miles an hour down a pathway that was all about success. Like a lot of people who either came from a sales background, or even a scarcity background, I measured success by the paycheck, the bank account, and the balance sheet. His question shifted my mindset because I learned that success, when measured by dollars and cents, can be fleeting. There is a laundry list of significant leaders in their industries who, at one time or another, experienced financial

83

bankruptcy and had to bounce back: Abraham Lincoln, Henry Ford, Milton Hershey, Donald Trump, H.J. Heinz, Francis Ford Coppola, even Stan Lee, the founder of Marvel comics.

Bouncing back from financial ruin requires clarity of purpose and focus. You have to be crystal clear about knowing your why and executing your strategy to achieve it.

You are either called to be a leader or you are not. You are either interested in making a significant impact on the lives of others, and helping them to do or to be their best, or you are not. What will you decide?

Practicing the Art
Deciding to Be a Leader

Getting clarity on why you choose to be a leader isn't always an easy thing. There are clues sprinkled throughout your life:
- Look back over the course of your life at the significant events that you have experienced. What events or experiences did you have that directed you toward the desire or knowing in your gut that you need to lead others?

Sometimes the reason we don't succeed is because we don't have the desire. Sometimes we don't succeed because we have the desire, but not the skills and the tools.
- Ask yourself this question: If you had the tools and the skills to effectively influence others to do or to be their best, on a scale of 1 to 10 (1 being low and 10 being extremely high) would you be a leader?

Once you've established that you have the desire be a leader, and you are willing to do whatever it takes to achieve your

CREATING YOUR LEADERSHIP STRATEGY

goal of leading, you just have to decide to take the actions to actually be a leader.

- Based on the answers to the previous questions, if you had to make a decision right now as to whether you will commit to doing whatever it takes to be a leader, how would you answer that question?

Now that you are committed, you need to be accountable to someone else that you will check in with about your progress.

- Select an accountability partner. Choose someone who would be willing to check in with you on your progress over the next two weeks so you can be held accountable for your commitment. Be sure to select a person who will not let you slide and tell you that it was okay to not honor your commitment, otherwise you are wasting your time and theirs.

PART II
MASTERING THE ART OF COACHING OTHERS

It's May 30, 2016. I am standing inside a 12th-century French church in Angoville-au-Plain, a few miles inland from Utah Beach in Normandy, France. I am staring at a bloodstained church pew. The stain has been there for a little over 73 years, and yet the story that tour guide is telling us is a story of two United States Army medics. Robert Wright and Kenneth Moore, from the 101st Airborne Division, were dropped behind enemy lines on June 6, 1944 before the landing of troops that would be known forever as D-day. The story our guide is telling isn't about how many enemy soldiers they killed that day, it's about how many soldiers they saved that day.

This small town was under siege for three days because it was a strategic point located between the landing zone at Utah Beach and a nearby road that led to Paris. The German Army needed to be stopped from utilizing this road to move troops and supplies between the two points. For three days the Allied troops exchanged control of the town with the German Army.

At one point Robert Wright and Kenneth Moore were told they were on their own as the American soldiers pulled back from the town. The first aid station set up inside the tiny church was left unprotected despite that it was filled with wounded soldiers. At times throughout these three days, German soldiers would enter the church, and seeing that both German and American soldiers were being treated, they would leave the two medics to do their work. Yes, these two young medics were treating German, American, and French soldiers who had been wounded. Years later in an interview, Kenneth Moore would tell his grandchildren that he saw his role as more of an observer and that he wasn't there to kill people.

For the three days, Wright and Moore risked their own lives as they continued to go outside the safety of the church and bring back more of the wounded so they could treat them.

CHAPTER 1

Outside the church is a gravestone with the Initials R.E.W., which stands for Robert E. Wright, who passed away on December 21, 2013. It was his wish to be buried there. His connection to this tiny little church stayed with him throughout his entire life, so it is befitting that it would be his final resting place. I am certain the events of those three days were ever present in the lives of those he saved seventy-three years earlier as well.

I have been working with leaders for more than seventeen years in one-on-one coaching or in a leadership development capacity. As a result of this, I have come to the conclusion that at some point in every leader's career there is a tipping point, call it a defining moment or a dark night of the soul, in which you have to dig deep inside and muster up all of your courage and do the right thing. This is the point at which a leader must put aside their self-centered needs and must focus on serving others.

Coaching is about putting aside your own needs as a leader and making others—your employees, your peers, your customers—the focus of your actions.

You can see coaching as a task, as a "thing" you do, or you can see it as a way to be...a way to be a leader.

CHAPTER 9

COACHING OTHERS & INFLUENCE

Coaching Defined

In a conversation with an HR Manager at one of my accounts about coaching, we were discussing the skills needed to be a great coach. I said that you have to be really good at listening and asking questions. So, he began to tell me a story about the best coach he had ever had—his high school football coach! Staying in the curious place, I asked him to tell me more about why he was such a great coach.

He shared how his coach was always pointing out to him how to improve. Whenever he was executing ineffectively, the coach would step in and show him exactly how to change and exactly how to do it. He explained that he had a short temper and that when he didn't execute a drill well, the coach would throw down his hat, start swearing, and make him do laps. I asked him, "Did he ever tell you when you did something right?" And he replied, "Of course he'd smack me in the helmet and pat me on the ass!" I was doing my best to not get triggered, and so I asked him another question: "How is being a high school sports coach like being an executive coach or a professional business coach?" His reply: "There is no difference, it's all the same!"

Can you imagine the line of employees outside the Human Resource Department waiting to file sexual harassment complaints because their leader patted their asses for completing a project on time or closing a deal?

CHAPTER 9

Two weeks prior to this conversation I had a similar conversation with an HR Manager at a different company. They were describing a great coaching session they had with an employee in which they gave the person a laundry list of ideas and suggestions to solve their problem for them. They went on to say that the person they were "coaching," "was taking pages and pages of notes because the advice I was giving them was so good!"

At that moment, all I could imagine was Yosemite Sam in a Bugs Bunny cartoon running in circles shouting, "Kill the Power, Kill the Power, Killllll the Powwwwwerrrrrr, dag nabbitt!"

These two examples clearly represent the overall lack of understanding and misinformation in the workplace today about what coaching is and what it isn't. I am going to be clear: **Giving advice is not coaching.** Sharing your experiences and passing on your wisdom to someone who is stuck sitting in the chair across listening to you because you are their boss is *not* coaching.

Feeling good about yourself because you gave them five pages of advice and all your great ideas on how you would handle things is *not* coaching. Telling someone exactly how to complete a task or what to do in a given situation is *not* coaching.

Twenty or so years ago when business coaching was gaining a deeper foothold in corporate America, many leaders and HR folks grabbed hold of the coaching jargon and started muddying up the waters by blurring the lines between coaching, mentoring, advice-giving, pontificating, preaching, lecturing, and thinking that they could fix an employee by changing them.

A lot of folks simply replaced the word coaching for everything they did with an employee. Maybe I am being a purist here, but there is a lot of stuff going on out there in the name of coaching that is anything *but* coaching!

92

Understanding Coaching & Influence

Like Leading, Coaching is an art. It requires knowing what brush (coaching skill) to use and when. It requires that you get out of the way and let the client or employee come to their own conclusions. Every single attribute of the Power vs. Force Model in Chapter 2 that was discussed in the context of Leadership, applies directly to Coaching as well. Coaching is a subset of Leadership. It is a way of "being" a leader.

For example, Coaching is not about you, it is about the other person. When you're giving advice, you may think it is about the other person but the truth is, that is about you and what you are thinking—not what they are thinking.

When you feel that the person you are Coaching is broken, you are holding them in a place of scarcity instead of abundance, Coaching is about believing that the other person is creative, resourceful, and whole. They are not some broken, wounded person with a defect that you can fix by sharing your vast knowledge and wisdom. You have to trust that this person has what it takes to find their own solutions to their problems. And accountability, ownership, and impact have to happen with them, not you.

When you approach coaching from a place of power instead of a place of force, you are showing up as an extremely powerful coach who influences and not a micromanager trying to control others.

Being an extraordinary leader means you are also an extraordinary Coach.

Now might be a good time to go back and review those differences to remind yourself of how you need to hold the coaching metaphor in your mind.

CHAPTER 9

Defining an Extraordinary Leader Who Coaches

So, how does all this play into your role as a leader? First, you have to understand that coaching is a way of *being* a leader and not something that is simply an action item, that you place on your to-do list. Coaching is a way of being a leader that sets up the structure for you to accomplish your purpose as a leader, which if you remember from the previous section is to...

Hold up a flashlight and sometimes a mirror so that others can see the obstacles they are placing on their paths, and then help them find solutions and actions to remove those obstacles. And, in doing this, they move farther down the path toward their ultimate purpose, goals, and objectives.

Through The Art of Asking Great Questions, each question or grouping of questions gives the coach a little more insight into what the other person believes or is thinking about a particular issue. It also allows the coach to direct the focus of the person they are coaching so that they can see the issue from a number of different perspectives. Remember, when you're telling, their mind is interpreting what you are saying through all of their filters and beliefs. What you don't know is whether or not they are comprehending your words in the same way that you intend them. Some of the biggest gaps between people are a result of one person misinterpreting what the other person is thinking. When you are asking questions, their mind has to focus on the question and respond.

The more questions you ask them, the broader a perspective they can have because your questions direct them to see the issue from a variety of different angles. The bigger the picture they can see, the better they are equipped to create their own solution to a particular challenge or problem.

Imagine one of your people is unable to see an obstacle on their

94

path. By asking questions, you are shining a light on the obstacle so they can see it more clearly and from a few different perspectives. Now they can see the obstacle and how it is getting in their way and preventing them from moving forward. That is what great Coaches do.

Leaders who Coach trust that their people are capable of doing their work and finding their own solutions to a problem and so they allow them to take responsibility for the results they produce. They know that their folks can creatively problem-solve and that they accomplish so much more when they are given the freedom and the opportunity to accomplish their work. Sometimes they just need a little help overcoming a blind spot or a different way to look at a particular issue so that they can make a better decision or find a different solution.

Leaders who Coach step back and create a space for their people to take a step forward. And in allowing this space, the employee can get a sense of purpose and meaning in their work because they are empowered to have a say in how their work gets done. They are invited to lean into their work and stretch beyond what's comfortable in order to grow their skills and their abilities. These team members grow far more than they ever could if the leader was doing all the heavy lifting and simply telling them what to do and how to do it.

It comes down to whether you as a leader trust your team to do their work, or if you have to place yourself at the center of the work and make it all about you.

For some of you this is going to feel like an oxymoron, a paradox, or a direct conflict to what you believe it means to be a leader or a coach, and that's okay!

Here is what I promise you: When you make the shift into being a leader who Masters the Art of Leading, Coaching, and Influencing, when you become a leader who truly Coaches others, your life will get much easier and you will significantly impact more people than you ever thought possible.

CHAPTER 9

Practicing the Art
What's your CQ (Coaching Quotient)?

Being a leader who coaches is a decision that you make each and every day. As with most things, it comes down to choices and you always have three:

1. Continue—You can choose to continue doing things the way that you are doing them and hope that things will get better.
2. Give Up (Quit)—You can pull back all together and do nothing and allow things to run their course.
3. Change—You can choose to do things differently. You can take one simple step toward being a leader.

Go back and review the results from the Influence Quotient (InQ) Assessment you completed at the end of Chapter 2. Review the results, knowing that the mindset you need to be a powerful Coach is aligned perfectly with the power side of the equation. Ask yourself again: What is the area you need to most focus on to be a more powerful Coach?

CHAPTER 10

THE A.R.T. OF THE QUESTION

Voltaire Was a Pretty Smart Guy

François-Marie Arouet, better known as Voltaire, was a prolific writer, historian, and philosopher. He was a staunch believer in freedom of religion and freedom of speech, so I find it ironic that the words he spoke some 300 years ago can set you free as a leader, coach, and influencer today.

He once said: "Judge a man by his questions rather than his answers." When it comes to The Art of Coaching Others, no truer words were spoken.

Many leaders feel the need to speak 80% of the time or more when they are engaged in conversations. They feel the need to have all the answers so they can guide the behaviors of their people in order to get what they want as quickly as possible. After all, they typically are very busy people.

I have spent countless coaching sessions with leaders who are frustrated and fed up with the fact that they have multiple conversations with their people and yet nothing changes. They talk *at* their people until they're blue in the face thinking that the more words they use, the more influential they are and the deeper they are embedding their message into the neuropaths of their employees' brains.

But, let me share with you a little secret: When you are talking

CHAPTER 10

at someone, their brain has a tendency to wander; the more you talk, the more you open your words up to their interpretations of what you are saying to them. The more you say, the more they interpret. Chances are, if they are in disagreement with what you're telling them, they are coming up with rebuttals along the way. You end up losing their attention because most people never pause to make sure the person they are communicating with is on the same page.

Again, think of the telephone message game, in which one person whispers a phrase into the ear of the person next to them. By the time you get to the end of the line (twenty people later) the message has been so distorted it is totally irrelevant. Picture that the next time you keep talking at your team members, and figure that every minute you talk nonstop represents one more person you're trying to pass the message through.

The other thing that happens when the other person isn't coming up with rebuttals or misinterpreting your message, is that they completely disengage themselves or distract themselves from the conversation because they are not actively participating. Not because they necessarily want to, but because you haven't given them a reason to be engaged.

Have you ever been engaged in a conversation with someone when they spoke *ad nauseum* and you totally checked out? Why? Well, your team members are no different, even if you believe that what you have to say is critically important, or you are the boss and that they have to or are supposed to listen. They're not!

If you are having a conversation with someone, especially when it is an uncomfortable topic like poor performance, chances are they will want to do everything in their power to get out of the conversation as quickly as possible. In those instances, they might just be agreeing to get out. Most people don't like feeling or being uncomfortable. If you want them to engage in a two-way interaction, you need to shift your approach from telling to asking.

Here's why:

Questioning Your Approach

During an exchange when the other person is being asked a question, it forces them to engage their brain and focus on the specific question or topic. This engages the pre-frontal cortex area of the brain where executive function takes place. Executive functions are the rational, reasoning, self-controlling, and self-managing functions needed to operate at a level required to make decisions and to lead others. Asking questions gives the person an opportunity to respond, as opposed to when you are making statements, especially if they perceive your statements as accusatory statements or threatening.

If you are having a tough conversation with an employee, and they start defending themselves or deflecting, they're probably acting out of the reptilian part of the brain, known as the amygdala, located near the base of the brain and the top of the spinal cord. The amygdala is associated with emotional responses—especially fear—and it plays a role in storing memories. The unconscious mind doesn't determine between emotional events that are happening in the current moment or one that happened twenty years ago. If an event someone is experiencing reminds them of a negative emotional event in which they were publicly embarrassed twenty years ago, you will get a negative response. This is why some people's responses around uncomfortable conversations or conflict are not always controlled. This inability to predict how the other person will respond is one reason why many leaders will avoid having these types of conversations.

You will know you're getting a negative response when one of two things unfold: a) the person gets defensive and pushes back aggressively (fight); or b) the person shuts down and disengages (flight). This happens when fear occurs and the person feels threatened. We will address this again in the next chapter when we discuss fear and how it shows up during coaching. For now, understand that a questioning approach is the key and accomplishes three very important things when coaching others:

CHAPTER 10

1. It engages the other person's brain and, therefore, engages them in a conversation.
2. It is a critical component in getting a person to focus on a particular topic so you can get them to move toward action and then ownership and accountability of those actions.
3. It increases the probability of success during your more challenging conversations because you are understanding their underlying beliefs and what is driving their behaviors instead of simply sharing your beliefs and telling them how to behave.

You have to engage a person and their brain if you want to influence them and experience any type of long-term change.

It is important to mention here that some folks, especially highly analytical ones, need more time to process before they respond. Other folks may take longer to respond depending on the perceived situation (safe or unsafe), what they are experiencing as they sit across from you, and the relationship between the two parties. Because of these factors, be sure not to rush your question process. Otherwise, they may feel like you are extracting data or performing a root canal instead of having a coaching conversation, and it will be a horrible exchange for the both of you.

The Art of Questioning Others

Asking great questions is an art. Questions have to be simple, well thought-out, and you have to be patient. The challenge for most leaders is that in coaching conversations they get impatient. Task-driven leaders may approach these types of conversations as an item to check off their to-do list. They may assume that they know what the other person is thinking and so they don't need to hear it from them. Finally, they might ask closed-ended questions that can be answered "yes" or "no," so they force the person to the conclusion or result they want. It's like a bad leadership scene from *The Office*.

THE A.R.T. OF THE QUESTION

It sounds something like this:

Leader: "Did you know you were missing the cover sheet on your TPS Reports?"

Employee: "No."

Leader: "Did you get the memo on the new cover sheet for the TPS Reports?"

Employee: "Yes..."

Leader: "Well make sure you read the memo and get it right next time."

Employee: "Okay..."

Leader: "Glad we had this chat!"

Employee: "Me, too."

Please don't confuse this with a coaching conversation to understand the other person's perspective or what happened; this is simply manipulating the other person to control them so you can get what you want.

Another type of interaction that happens with leaders who are impatient or don't like silence is to ask questions, and when they don't get an immediate response, they attempt to answer the question for the other person by giving them choices or extrapolating on the question. Again, this is manipulative, even though the facade is meant to look as if the leader is supporting the employee and trying to help.

It sounds something like this:

Leader: "So I was wondering why you took the flux capacitor and moved it to the other side of the room?"

Employee: "Wellllllllll..." (or dead silence)

Leader: "Was it because you thought that is what needed to happen, or was it because you weren't sure what to do? Did you think about how it would impact others? Or did you not even consider the impact on the rest of the team? Why didn't you ask for my input? You know you can always ask me for help if you need it!"

101

CHAPTER 10

Employee: "Well I thought..."

Leader: "You know you can talk to me, I will listen because my door is always open, just tell me what you need! This was a great conversation and don't forget I am here for you, just let me know how I can help."

Employee: "Wow, thanks again for your help, I always feel so much better after our chats!"

Overexaggeration, maybe...however, some rendition of this conversation happens more times than you may believe.

Another important factor to consider when asking great questions is the size and dimension of the question. You could see in the previous example that the specificity of the question and the eventual narrowing down of the question as the leader drove them toward the specific response they were seeking. The Art of the Question is always about starting off with questions that are big, vague, and general in nature.

Questions like:
- So what happened?
- That sounds interesting...what happened?
- Can you help me understand what happened?
- How are things going?
- Can you say more about that?

These questions allow the person being coached to go anywhere they want to go in the conversation. One of the biggest mistakes a leader can make is when they think they know what is going on in the brain of the employee. In fact, a great many leaders pride themselves on the idea that they do know. The truth of the matter is that you don't have a clue what's going on in another's mind, you can only project your own thoughts and ideas onto them. And, yes, that would be your ego getting in the way of truly understanding what the person is thinking, their thought process, or their approach to the issue.

When it comes to influencing others through the coaching model, you need to take into consideration the Beliefs, Behaviors, & Results Model we discussed at the end of Part I on page 79.

If you want to influence your employees to change and sustain that change, you have to understand what they actually believe about something. You can't do that by trying to guide their thought process, or get them to respond in a specific way that is simply reflective of your beliefs.

Taking the time to understand what the person is thinking seems like a lot of work in the short-term, but the long-term payoff is extremely high, because you are influencing their beliefs and what they think. If you can get those aligned, the behaviors and results will follow.

It is better to ask more questions in a staged process by asking smaller questions that are general in nature, than it is to hit a grand slam home run with one big question that can be confusing to hear and difficult to answer. It is much easier for the other person to digest, and it allows them to share in any direction and helps you to understand how they think. Notice the difference between these two approaches:

Approach A:
- So, tell me how you're progressing in regard to the timeline for the Zenith project, any problems? Are we going to deliver on time? What can I do to help?

Approach B:
- So, what's happening with the Zenith Project? (Wait for the response)
- Anything I need to know? (Wait for the response)
- How do you feel about the delivery date? (Wait for the response)
- Need anything?

CHAPTER 10

More Powerful Than a Locomotive

I was working with a Fortune 100 client for a couple of years. Not long ago he made the decision to take his team through our Leadership Development Program, *The Art of Leading, Coaching, & Influencing Others™*. During one of our group coaching calls with his team, he shared this story:

> *"Joe I have to tell you, I am finally and totally a firm believer in The Art of Asking Questions. We were presenting a new program to the C-Suite and a few of the VPs. Things weren't going too well. People were pushing back and getting a little argumentative, and so I completely switched gears.*
>
> *I just started asking questions—questions that helped everyone in the room understand and get to what the underlying beliefs and concerns were. The whole meeting shifted. By asking questions, I took what could have been a total and complete disaster and turned it into an incredibly productive meeting. Even our CIO complimented us on the results."*

I shared this story with you because I think it demonstrates what happens when you engage people in the conversation by asking questions. And it doesn't matter if it is a 1-on-1 situation or a 1-on-20. It doesn't matter if you're facilitating a group, having a one-on-one coaching session, or engaging an audience in a presentation. People have a normal tendency to push back on information that is being presented to them, whether it is because they don't like change, they're looking for a reason why you are wrong and they are right, they want to control everything, or any other reason that is about them and not about you.

When you ask questions, you invite the others involved into the discussion space where you can learn more about their underlying beliefs, and that gives you a higher probability of influencing them to change, accept, take action, or buy in.

104

THE A.R.T. OF THE QUESTION

The most important thing to remember is that asking questions is truly an art and something you need to practice if you really want to be a great leader, a great coach, and a powerful influencer. And yet, you will meet obstacles along the way...

CHAPTER 11

GREMLINS: MOVING THROUGH THE FEAR F.I.L.L.E.R.S.™

If you are going to be a leader who coaches, you are going to run into what coaches refer to as "gremlins." These are the voices that sit on your shoulder and the shoulder of the people you are coaching so they can whisper all kinds of negative things into your ear to stop you from taking action. This is also what Steven Pressfield, in his brilliant book, *The War of Art*, refers to as "resistance."

When you examine procrastination, inaction, stuckness, dumbing down, putting things off, avoidance, push back, the timing is not quite right, and anything else you want to call it...you will find fear lurking in the background.

Just like we each are 100% responsible for the results we are creating in our own lives, we are each 100% responsible for our own gremlins and the results that occur as a consequence. Typically gremlins prevent you and me from achieving what we set out to achieve.

If you find that you are working extremely hard in a coaching conversation, harder than the person you're coaching, then you are probably hooked emotionally or you're making it all about you. Meaning that your gremlin is getting in the way. It could also be that you are attempting to coach the other person's gremlin and that is what is getting in the way and creating friction.

CHAPTER 11

Gremlins? Say What?

Gremlins can offer quite a smorgasbord of destructive and useless phrases. Some of these phrases have been learned from your past experiences and some of them were passed onto you from friends and family.

Gremlins whisper in your ear phrases like:
- "You are not enough."
- "This is a stupid idea."
- "Who do you think you are?"
- "You never could handle the stress."
- "Getting a little big for your britches."
- "You're...
    - ...too old."
    - ...too young."
    - ...not pretty enough."
    - ...not smart enough."
    - ...not skinny enough."
    - ...not tall enough."
    - ...not short enough."
    - ...etc.

Basically, gremlins are internal fears being verbalized inside your head. Sometimes they are screaming, and sometimes they are soft whispers that lures you into a state of inaction, status-quo, rationalization, or avoidance. The bigger the fear, the bigger the gremlin; the bigger the action, the bigger the gremlin.

This would be a pretty crazy world if you walked around and heard the voices inside of everyone else's head inside your own head. Years ago Mel Gibson starred in a movie called *What Women Want*, where he could hear the thoughts going on inside of womens' heads. While it made for a good movie (according to some), it revealed the

108

breadth of insecurities that in reality, both men and women struggle with on a daily basis.

The truth is that we all battle our internal gremlins, and that is more the norm than the exception. That thought should help you understand others more, especially when coaching others to help move beyond their fears and stretch beyond their comfort zones — or as we refer to in the world of coaching — to *play bigger.*

As a leader, your job is to manage your gremlins. I say manage because the fact is that your gremlins never really go away. The famous Academy Award-winning actor Henry Fonda, continued to throw up before he performed, even at the age of 75. Whether they are your gremlins, or they are hitched to the wagon of the people you lead, gremlins never disappear, they just get smaller.

Gremlins and Fear

As I mentioned earlier, behind the voices of the gremlin is fear. Fear of success, failure, embarrassment, the truth, and even at times reality. Sometimes we just aren't willing to face the truth about ourselves.

The good news is, that most people can agree upon the fact that 85% of the things we worry about or fear, never happen. Don Joseph Goeway, in his book, *The End of Stress,* references the study behind this fact. He goes on to say that of those things that do happen, 79% of the folks discovered they could handle the difficulty better than expected, or they learned a valuable lesson worth learning. According to Goeway, that equates to the fact that 97% of what you worry about is nothing more than unsubstantiated fear.

In other words, most of the fear that we allow our gremlins to stir up is based on a faulty premise because the odds are whatever it is we are afraid of isn't going to happen!

The probability of your career coming to a crashing halt because one of your people missed a deadline is basically nonexistent. Especially

CHAPTER 11

if you and your team have delivered results on time over and over and over again. And yet, this is one of my client's gremlins they shared with me during a coaching session.

The power a gremlin usurps comes from the magnifying effect that fear has when we allow it to take over our thoughts and then our emotions, and allow it to build. We have a thought; we think about all the things that could happen that are not good.

Why? Because we have and continue to be programmed throughout our lives from a fear-based perspective. It starts at an early age with your parents, who, for the most part, are trying to keep you safe: "Don't you ever wander away from me on a busy street ever again!" Over time, as your exposure to the media increases, you find that to sell more advertising and products, the media and institutions leverage fear...fear...and sex. You can't sell any advertising if nobody is paying attention.

There is a reason why a beautiful model-like news reporter is telling you to watch the six o'clock news because your house might be infested with Boo-ba-la-caca, the newest deadly, toxic mold that was recently discovered in the rainforest of the Amazon. And, yes, it might be lurking in your home preying on you, your pets, and your innocent children. Never mind that you live in a desert...you shop on Amazon, and yet, you've never been to the Amazon. But your life and the life of your family is now in grave danger? Really? And yet it never is, is it?

Fear is also at the root of all the drug commercials telling you you're sick and creating a society of drug-dependent addicts that believe a drug, hot chocolate, and therapy will reduce your anxiety because your presidential candidate lost the race.

When you have a fearful thought and you allow it to take a few laps around the track rather than noticing it and letting it pass, it grows stronger and gains speed until you find yourself spinning out of control and leaning toward the irrational, fearful side of the equation. Your molehill is now Mt. Everest and you're frozen on the summit, paralyzed, unable to move.

Overcoming Fear: The FEAR F.I.L.L.E.R.S.™

Fear is almost always associated with a loss of some sort. The spectrum of loss can be extremely wide, ranging anywhere from losing a few dollars at the church carnival on a game, or losing your life in an accident. The trick is to make sure you don't confuse one end of the range with the other. Once you can come to the truth about what you're actually dealing with, you can begin to move forward and actually make better decisions.

If you can agree that fear is associated with loss, then what follows is a process to help you overcome your fears and then, in turn, use this process with your team members who may be paralyzed by their own gremlins and not moving forward.

The Fear F.I.L.L.E.R.S.™ Process has three parts to it, and each part refers to a question you need to ask yourself or the person you are coaching. The process is designed to move you from an irrational, emotional state to a state that has been processed through a more rational and logical approach.

Step 1 — Question 1: *What am I afraid of losing?*

This question is designed to help you identify what it is that you believe you will lose as a result of this action, inaction, etc. This leads us to the actual F.I.L.L.E.R.S.™ which is an acronym that stands for the following:

F — **Freedom** — This includes freedom of choice, financial freedom, or being controlled by someone else (their boss, a committee, the organization or institution, etc.). For those of us who like to be in control, this can pose an extremely big issue. A person who likes to be in control may feel threatened or that they are at risk of losing their freedom. Someone with authority issues will certainly bump up against this rather frequently.

I — **Income** — This one of the fillers is extremely powerful because it has to do with money. Money is one of the most powerful forces in the world and lines up right alongside power and

CHAPTER 11

sex. It also shows up on the lower levels of Maslow's Hierarchy and impacts a person's ability to provide for themselves and their family. Depending on your background and how you were raised, this can be an extremely powerful motivator and loss of it can cause extreme reactions or fears.

L — **Love** — This has to do with relationships and can vary anywhere from a casual friendship at work to the loss of a significant relationship like a spouse or a child. The whole idea of not being loved for who we are can play into the "not enough" syndrome discussed in Chapter 3. This is why some people stay in relationships that are unhealthy, whether they are personal or business. It is out of a desire to be loved and accepted, and ties into our innate human desire to belong.

L — **Life** — This filler can be real or imagined. While I addressed earlier that fear can be a good thing because it protects us from making bad choices that could actually endanger our lives, it can also be imagined. How many times have you heard someone say they would rather die than speak publicly, or if they had to confront an employee about a performance issue? Of course, as a leader they would never admit this, but it is part of the dialogue in some leaders' heads. This can be seen on teams or in departments where bad behavior is tolerated and the leader does absolutely nothing to address it out of a fear of facing the conflict by having the difficult conversation.

E — **Ego** — This is what you believe about yourself. An ego is a tricky thing; it represents your internal personal identity to self, it includes self-respect, self-importance, self-esteem, etc. People with big or overinflated egos can come across as arrogant and filled with false pride. Typically they are covering up a low sense of self-worth. On the other end of the spectrum, you may find folks that act like doormats because their sense of self-worth is so low that they don't believe they matter. These may be two sides of the same coin, and connects to what was discussed in Chapter 3. The important thing to remember is that what you believe about yourself plays a big role in how you navigate fear, especially when you feel that your sense of self-worth is being threatened and you need to save yourself.

R — Reputations — This filler is a close cousin to the ego as it is the outward persona (sometimes known as the "mask") we feel we have to manage. It can also be considered our personal or professional brand or our promise. In other words, what can someone expect to experience as a result of interacting with you? You know what you get when you pop open a red can with the letters Coca-Cola® on it. Some folks are so wrapped up in their reputation that they make all their decisions based on what other people will do or think of them. Think about politicians whose opinions change with the polls. Delivering a consistent and positive experience to the people that you interact with is important. Where you can get into trouble here is when the image that you are projecting outward is inconsistent with who you are. If your sole focus is to control what others think of you, you are in for a roller coaster ride of ups and downs. The truth is you can't control what everyone thinks about you, so don't try.

S — Security — This filler encompasses a wide range of areas and may even overlap some of the fillers listed above. Where you get your sense of security, whether money, freedom, shelter, family, career, a nestegg, faith, or whatever or whomever you choose, will have a powerful impact on how you navigate through fear. Abraham Maslow referred to safety and security as the second level of human needs right above food, warmth, and water. It is important. When we place our own sense of security in things that are temporary, and, everything is temporary, fear can become an elusive demon that never lets us rest. I made the choice long ago that my freedom was critical to my happiness and that I was willing to risk throwing away a very healthy six-figure position with a great benefits package and the false sense of security that comes from working for a Fortune 50 company to start my own business. My sense of freedom trumped my sense of security. Fear of losing my freedom was more fearful to me than losing money or what appeared to be a secure job.

Once you have identified each and every filler, then you have to ask yourself the second question, which is:

Step 2 — Question 2: *What is the truth?*

Answering this question will help you to identify whether fear is steeped in reality or if it is based on a faulty premise. Sometimes our fear causes us to think irrationally as it overruns our thought process. Believing that you will be fired for a slight mistake is irrational. Another aspect of asking yourself what is the truth is that you may find that the risk versus the reward of taking this action may be too high. There is a big difference between deciding to have a difficult conversation with an employee and bungee jumping from a crane off a bridge in the Democratic Republic of the Congo. Once you have interjected a more rational approach to the risk-reward equation, you can move to the next action. Either you say no and end the internal discussion right there, or you move toward action, which leads you to the next question, which is:

Step 3 — Question 3: *What is the next logical action I need to take to move forward?*

The next logical step is whatever moves you forward. It can be a leap or a baby step. Just start moving forward. Don't wait another second, even if it is a small action, take it and get the momentum going.

It should be emphasized that fear is not all bad. Fear can keep us from making poor decisions and minimizing risk, and it can prevent you or someone who works for you from getting the results they are capable of, or living the life they want.

Business is all about managing risk. It requires that you carefully weigh the upside and the downside of each decision. A very dear mentor of mine, Dr. Nido Qubein, shared with me this simple process for making great business decisions and it applies here as well. He said when you are faced with a big decision and you're not sure what to do, ask yourself these three questions:

1. What's the best thing that can happen as a result of your decision/action?
2. What's the worst thing that can happen as a result of your decision/action?
3. Can you live with the worst thing that can happen?

If the answer is yes, move forward. If the answer is no, drop it and move on or run it through the FEAR F.I.L.L.E.R.S.™ Process just to be sure you're not cheating yourself out of something that is important because your gremlin is running amuck. This applies to you and to the people you are coaching.

Coaching Your Folks...Not Their Gremlins

In a coaching relationship it is important that you don't get stuck coaching your people's gremlins. If they are spinning in their fear, you're not going to get very far because gremlins are not coachable. You will simply end up being extremely frustrated. If you are emotionally hooked into their drama or yours, you cannot truly coach because coaching requires being other-centered. When you are hooked in to emotional drama, you start worrying about self-preservation and making sure that you are addressing your needs, and that diverts you from your ability to focus on the other person. You become self-centered

CHAPTER 11

and focused on getting the results you want, or you are headed down a path trying to corral their gremlin. You simply cannot tame, corral, control, or terminate anyone's gremlin other than your own.

This is why asking questions is critical to being a great coach. You can't talk someone out of their fear because no matter how rational you are, they are not. You will know if you're hooked, or stuck, when the coaching becomes difficult and it seems like you are working way too hard to move the other person forward.

Sometimes when you get stuck during a coaching conversation, a great technique to move a person forward is to ask them the question from the perspective of a third person, who isn't wrapped up in their fear. It gives them a little breathing room and takes the heat off of them in the moment. Sometimes they are so wrapped up that you need to help them step out of themselves, but stay in the room.

It might sound something like this:

- "So what would a leader who knew what needed to happen in a situation like this do...?"
- "If the roles were reversed, what would you tell me to do in this situation?"
- "Do you consider yourself a good leader? What would a good leader do in a situation like this?"
- "If this were one of your direct reports, what would you say to them?"

The idea is to frame the situation in a way that moves the person a half-of-a-step back from the uncomfortable feelings so they can see it from a slightly different view. A view that isn't so close to the pressure they are feeling at the moment.

Being a coach who influences means that you have the ability to self-manage your way through the fear paradigm...yours and theirs. The FEAR F.I.L.L.E.R.S.™ Process is a great tool to help you manage your way through fear a bit better.

116

Practicing the Art
Freedom from Fear

1. Make a list of three things you've put off but really want to do. Never mind the reason or rationalization behind why you haven't done them yet, just list them.
2. Go back through the Fear F.I.L.L.E.R.S.™ in this chapter and identify all of the things that you fear losing (freedom, income, etc.) associated with these actions.
3. Knowing that 97% of the things you fear never happen, rank order these items based on urgency and importance. In other words, which of these (and the time constraints associated with it) is the most important to you? For example, trekking to Mount Everest base camp is best tackled the younger you are.
4. Make a selection and build a timeline of events that need to happen in order for you to accomplish your goal.
5. Call a friend or partner with whom you can share your goal. Commit to accomplishing this action, and ask them to hold you accountable and check in with you on your progress.

(Note: When referring to fear in this chapter I am excluding psychological illnesses like Post Traumatic Stress Disorder (PTSD), Depression, or any other types of mental illness.)

CHAPTER 12
VICTIMHOOD & THE POWER OF CHOICE

The Victim Mentality

As a leader, at some point in your career you are going to encounter an employee who believes they are a victim and acts this out in the workplace. As a society we have moved toward a lack of responsibility and ownership for the results we create in our lives. At the time of this writing, an average known comedian posted photos of herself holding a bloodied mask of the President of the United States, and then through a turn of publicity events, turned around and screamed victim for the damage he did to her career after she received some backlash for the photo. Yes this is news, and no, you can't make this stuff up!

But to confuse an ignorant publicity event gone bad with a real-life tragic event seems like a travesty. Everyday, people around the world become innocent victims of crimes, acts of war, and terrorism. These folks have legitimate reasons to call themselves victims. Confusing an ignorant publicity stunt gone bad with a real life tragedy is a travesty, in my opinion. And yet, regardless of the cause or situation, be it real or imagined, everyone has a choice in how they respond.

This begs the questions:
- Why is it that some people choose to rise above a traumatic, life-changing, event and move past it? Many times even stronger or better for having experienced the event?

CHAPTER 12

- Why is it that some people get dragged down into the quagmire of negative, painful emotions or thoughts for years and are unable to move forward?
- Why is it that some people create false drama and pretense that allow them to avoid responsibility, accountability, and ownership for their work, by playing the victim card over and over and over again?

I want to clarify that there are people who are clinically depressed or suffer from some type of personality disorder that will not allow them to overcome certain challenges or issues. In fact, there is an entire segment of science known as victimology that goes into great length to understand victims. However, for our purposes, when I am speaking of a victim mentality, I am speaking of the third type, the false drama, which shows up in the workplace that leaders must face.

I'm referring to the situations in which someone fails to take responsibility for the results they are creating in their life. This is the person who creates and stirs up drama like a black cloud that follows them everywhere they go. It occurs in situations with friends, family, or even total strangers.

I'm speaking of the person who always has someone else to blame or point a finger for why they can't be happy, have success, or be a team player because they blame their parents, their peers, or their kindergarten teacher who yelled at him and shredded his paper because he colored the flowers green. For the record, I eventually did prove her wrong...I just didn't know that the Cymbidium Orchid was green when I was five years old.

Most leaders will shy away from dealing with these types of situations in the hope that it will go away, or they will diminish the impact the victim's behavior is having on the rest of the team. As a leader, if you fail to address these types of situations in a timely manner, you may find yourself being a victim of an employee who is hell-bent on filing a complaint against you—or worse, filing a lawsuit because they feel they were wronged.

VICTIMHOOD & THE POWER OF CHOICE

As a leader, you may ask yourself...what on earth could anyone be getting from playing the victim over and over? As much as you may not understand the answer to that question, your job as a leader and a coach is to have patience enough so that you can ask enough questions in order to help them get to a place where they can see it. That is, if they are willing to look at it long enough to decide to change or for you to take the necessary actions to move them on down the road.

To start, it helps if you understand the basic premise that most behaviors, regardless of whether the behavior is positive or negative, serves the person in some way. In other words, we all get something from our actions, whether we are conscious and aware of it, or we are unconscious and unaware.

Remember what is driving those behaviors and work to get behind the behavior to understand why they think that way. That is the only way to help a person uncover the belief and open themself up to the possibility of reframing the belief so that they can achieve different, more positive results.

However, sometimes the victim-minded people are so buried in the role, that they fail to see that they are getting anything from being a victim. The truth is they are getting something from the behavior, but it isn't what they think they are getting. In fact, like many things in coaching, the behavior the person you are coaching is exhibiting is giving them the exact opposite results of what they want. Your job as a coach is to try to help them see the truth about what they are doing. An employee with a victim mentality or belief system might believe that if they create drama and magnify the situation, it will get them attention. They may believe that they will get sympathy and people will step in and console them or let them back out of their responsibilities because they are struggling and suffering so greatly.

Again, I am not talking about legitimate situations or circumstances, I am talking about the person who has an excuse for everything and fails to see how they are creating and recreating the same result in their life over and over again. The Universal Law of Reciprocity, spoken of by Emerson, also known as "reaping what you sow," will

121

guarantee that creating drama will bring even more drama into your life. As you attract more drama and lack of responsibility, you will attract more people that align with those beliefs. If you are a leader that plays the victim, you will end up attracting and being surrounded by like minds who will play out this incredibly destructive and demoralizing behavior.

Getting Unstuck: Holding The Mirror

I was working with a client a few years ago who was stuck in their victimhood. They were passed over for a promotion more times than a broken vehicle at the Indy 500, and so you would think that they would have experienced a wake-up call. Nope...in his world of virtual reality, the reasons he was passed over according to his belief system were:

A. His boss didn't like him.
B. His boss avoided conflict and therefore didn't appreciate his straightforwardness and ability to cut to through the crap and "Call'em like I see'em!"
C. His boss's boss didn't really know him; he hadn't had enough exposure to her.
D. His weekly 5-hour staff meetings were to keep everyone on track and not about control and micromanaging.
E. His peers who did get promoted simply knew the right people, although he wished them the very best and had no ill-will toward any of them.
F. Everything he did was for his people and his team!
G. Since no one was promoting him, he needed to be seen in the best possible light, so he self-promoted at every possible opportunity.

However, this was the reality others saw and experienced when dealing with him. This was his brand:

A. His boss tolerated this employee and was well aware of the person he was in front of his people and the inauthentic person he was in front of the boss.
B. His boss didn't like conflict. She tolerated him because he had been with the company for such a long time and was a part of the old guard.
C. His boss's boss actually was quite aware of him and knew he had some challenges but he got results.
D. His 5-hour staff meetings were actually a complete waste of time because they could have been handled via email as they were simply updates and status reports.
E. His peers got promoted because they were good leaders and made their success about the team and not only about themselves.
F. Everything he did was about himself.
G. He was an overbearing, self-promoting, inauthentic leader who wasn't fooling anyone.

From a coaching perspective it is important to be self-aware enough and to manage your thoughts so that you are not judging the person I described above as being, bad, broken, or needing to be fixed. What they need from you as their leader and their coach is to hold up a mirror for them long enough so they can see the reality of what they are creating in their life. Chances are, what they are creating is not what they want, they just don't see it and/or they don't know another way. If you were coaching this person, you would need to create an opportunity to help them get out of their own way. One place to start is by giving them choices.

Getting to Choices

You can't start off with telling them what you see...that isn't important... yet. You need to start off with general, vague questions and gently take them down a path toward uncovering the reality of the situation. When

CHAPTER 12

someone is blinded and unable to see, removing the blindfold off of their eyes when they didn't ask you to, or they are not ready to see any issues, can hurt, and so sometimes you need to be patient, go slowly, and remember it is a process.

Below is one way of approaching someone who is stuck or has a victim mindset:

- So how do you think things are going?
- On a scale of 1 to 10 (with 1 being low and 10 being high), how would you rate yourself as a leader? As a developer of people? On your promote-ability? Choose whatever the focus of your conversation needs to be. This method of applying a number to an issue helps take what is usually a very subjective concept and move it into a more objective perspective.
- When they answer, help them to explain it in detail by following up with questions so they can create a mental image in their mind and yours. It has to be their picture, their thoughts, and their vision, NOT YOURS! Yours doesn't matter if you can't, don't, or won't see theirs.
- Use questions like:
  - Can you say more about that?
  - What would that look like?
  - How would that change things for the better? Worse?
  - What would the impact be? On you? Your team? Your peers?
  - How would that make things better?

At some point with a person who has a victim mindset you have to shift into a close-up image of themselves in the mirror. When they start interjecting the faults or actions of others, or if they deflect the question by pointing in another direction, you have to be able to take it back to them. This is where you ask more questions like:

- I'm not sure why you are talking about Bob, we're having a discussion about you and your leadership?

124

VICTIMHOOD & THE POWER OF CHOICE

- I'm not sure how that person or situation has anything to do with our discussion about your leadership? Your job? Your results?
- What have you noticed about each situation we discussed? In other words, who has consistently been involved in each situation?
- Have you noticed that each time I look for who owns this, you point to everyone other than yourself?

Then get them to step in and try on what it might be like to take ownership for the issue:

- So what if you were to take responsibility for the results you're getting (or not getting) in your work? What would that look like?
- What if you took full responsibility for what is happening with your job? Your work? Your team?

The next step is to move toward actions and possible solutions that are measurable, achievable, and that you can clearly track, and answer the question with a simple yes or no.

- If you were to take 100% ownership for the results you are getting...what would need to happen?
- What would that look like?
- What actions would you need to take?

When they give you a possible answer, no matter how crazy it seems, count it and add it to the mix. You may get responses like:

- I could quit.
- You could fire me.
- I could fire all of my people.
- I could abuse the system and go on intermittent FMLA and pretend I am incapable of working because I am stressed, especially on Mondays and Fridays!

CHAPTER 12

No matter what they say, reply with:
- That's a possibility, what's another one (hold up one finger and start counting the responses)?
- That's great, what would another one be?
- And another?
- And another? (Keep pushing until you get a minimum of 3 actions...the more the better)!

Sometimes the person will stop after one and say, I really don't know or I have no idea. If you by chance get the infamous responsibility shirking, dumbing down, escape line of:

"I DON'T KNOW!"

- You respond with a Powerful Question. What if you did know? What would your answer be?
- If you did know, what would you say?
- And if for a moment we sprinkled magic dust on you and knew the answer...what would you say?
- And if we were just brainstorming a few ideas about what you could do...what would you say?

The truth is more than likely, they do know, they just don't want to have to take action, or they may believe that the behavior or the results were okay because you avoided having the conversation for so long and left it untouched, so of course they would believe it was okay. That is why addressing performance or unacceptable behavior is so important to do as soon as it happens.

The key idea here is that you are helping them to create choices. The more choices, the better. You see, victims feel like they have no choice. They believe they have been burdened, that they are stuck, and that it's not their fault. They are where they are because it is everyone else's fault and so we need to help them see that they are stuck because they choose to be stuck.

126

Empowering Others

Your focus here should be helping them see that they can empower themselves to get unstuck and move forward. They can choose to take action or they can stay stuck. They can shift or change, or they can choose to lose their job.

Having choices empowers people because not only do they create the choices, they get to choose one, two, or all. There is a fundamental shift that happens when someone awakens to the idea that they are creating their own stuck behavior and they have the ability to get unstuck.

Hopefully at this point you will have at least five fingers in the air, which means there are at least five possible actions for them to take. This is a good time to summarize the choices and then ask the person which ones seem to be the best choices. Questions like:

- Which ideas seem to be the best choices?
- Which one(s) do you think make the most sense?
- If you see three good choices, ask them: Which of these three ideas makes the most sense? Would be the best choice?

Once you get them to choose an option or options, be sure not to overload them with 10 action items, anywhere from 1 to 3 works depending on the situation, then move them into establishing a time frame and getting them to commit.

- So what you committed to doing is x, y, and z, is that right?
- So that we are on the same page, you agreed to do x, y, and z, are you in agreement?
- Let's see if I have this, you agreed to x, by next Thursday, did I get that?

Next, create an avenue for them to communicate their progress back to you so that you can hold the person accountable. It is important that the onus of reporting back or following up is on them and not on you. It is not your job to track them down to find out whether they succeeded or failed.

CHAPTER 12

This can be done with simple questions like:
- So how will I know you have accomplished what we agreed upon?
- So how will I know you succeeded?
- What would be a good way to inform me that you are on track?

What you are looking for here is email, stop by, call you, or some form of conversation. I prefer a face-to-face if possible so I can ask questions to find out what worked, what didn't, or what the impact was on them or the other members of the team.

If you get a response like:
- Well, you could call me next Thursday to check in.
- You could email me sometime to see how I am doing.
- You could stop by my office sometime and ask me how I am doing.

Respond with:
- That is a possibility and what might be another way that would place the responsibility on you?
- That is an option and what would be another idea that would let me know that you did what we agreed upon?

When you have the follow-up meeting, be curious about how it unfolded, the results, and, when they succeed, give them praise for being successful. The whole idea here is to remember that this is a process and we are looking for some movement in the right direction. The goal is to get them moving in the right direction and hopefully this process will achieve that goal. Helping them see the positive impact their changes are having on the team and/or their career will certainly help move them in that direction.

Webster defines the word *empower* as "giving someone the authority or power to do something." It can also be defined as making

VICTIMHOOD & THE POWER OF CHOICE

someone stronger and more confident, especially in controlling their rights. The original meaning of the prefix *em* means "to be"—and of course—power. *To be in power.*

As their leader you are helping the person *to be in power* of their own outcomes. This concept of empowering people was the original purpose of the U.S. Constitution.

We have sadly been transformed into a society of victims where the government and institutions tell us we need them to take care of us and that we are victims. The new norm is that if we are unhappy or if we don't like something it is not our fault, it is the democrats, the republicans, the Chinese, Muslims, or somebody else. And yet, this victim mentality shows up in the workplace and you as a leader must learn to deal with it.

Coaching your team can be seen as another thing to do on your to-do list or a painstaking process you have to endure. You can see this as a "soft skills" approach to babying your team, or you can see it as a privilege.

The privilege of helping others break the chains that bind them and keep them enslaved to old behaviors and beliefs that don't serve them any longer is the freedom from the belief that they are helpless victims, reliant on institutions (or someone other than themselves) to break themselves free and start achieving the success they deserve.

Victims lack purpose because they have no hope and no vision to strive toward. It's been said that without vision (purpose) the people will perish. Remember leadership is not a reward for performance...it is a privilege...it is a calling.

CHAPTER 13

ACCOUNTABILITY, PUSHBACK, & CURING THE DIS-EASE

Most leaders feel that the weight of the world is resting on their shoulders. They want to be successful and so they work long and hard. They commit themselves to their team and at times make great sacrifices for them. If a person has been promoted to a leadership position for the first time, they are susceptible to doing more than they should because they may feel like they have been given an opportunity and they don't want to blow it.

A leader must learn the subtle art of putting the accountability, ownership, and impact where it belongs. What they don't need to do is shoulder the responsibility for their people and weigh themselves down with a cage of monkeys on their back.

Addressing The Dis-ease...Not the Symptom

Your job as a leader who coaches is to shine the light, paint the picture, and help others see how they are getting in their own way. In doing that, you will free others up so they can tap into their inner strengths, talents, and brilliance, and then follow their path toward higher levels of engagement, clarity, and purpose. In other words, you are helping others create happiness and success.

CHAPTER 13

As we discussed throughout this book (and more in depth in Chapter 2), The Art of Leading, Coaching, and Influencing is most impactful when you are asking questions for all the following reasons:

- You engage their brain and allow them to think through the problem to the solution.
- You give them a sense of ownership and teach them they have the answers to their own questions or challenges.
- They feel empowered and you give them a sense of purpose at work, which, in turn, promotes self-worth and value.
- You can guide them and give them insight into how they may approach a challenge by asking questions without telling them what or how to do something.
- You are grooming them to be coaches and leaders by teaching them (through your actions) how an effective leader develops their team members.

With all those benefits, why would anyone not shift from telling and statements to asking and questions? Because it takes time and many people push back. Some leaders do everything they can to avoid difficult conversations. They may talk in a roundabout way, but never nail down the real conversation that needs to take place—the real conversation that addresses the dis-ease instead of attempting to talk about the symptoms; meanwhile the dis-ease keeps ravaging the team, productivity, or morale.

Your job as a coach is to get past the fluff by getting to the core issue. This takes time, this takes patience, this takes the ability to self-manage and stay unhooked and out of the nitty gritty details so you can focus on the bigger picture.

I was working with a leader who had someone on his team who always had to be right, to be the smartest person in the room. They referred to her as "Nurse No" because no matter what idea or suggestion someone else offered, their answer was always "NO!" Why? Because she always had the right answer, it felt good to be right, she held the belief that it made her look good in front of her peers and that it was appreciated. Besides, it made her feel important and valued on the inside to know she was smart—the smartest person in the room.

The truth was nobody liked Nurse No, she had the reputation as being difficult to work with, and while she believed everyone appreciated her mental prowess, people actually disliked having her on the team. The leader attempted to have various conversations with Nurse No by telling her what to do or how to change, but these didn't work. Nothing changed until her leader was willing to have the real coaching conversation about the real results she was getting.

The funny thing about this situation was that during the conversation to address the real issue, there was a point where Nurse No came to the realization about how self-centered she was being and how her need to be right was driving people away. The leader than asked a question she knew the answer to, which was, "Does the behavior you're exhibiting, remind you of anyone?" You would have thought you had stabbed her in the forehead with a knitting needle. "Oh my God!" A light bulb went off when she realized that she was acting exactly like another leader with whom she really struggled and actually couldn't stand.

The magic of this conversation was that it allowed Nurse No to realize the full impact of her behavior. She saw what it was costing her and how it was damaging her reputation, the same way she saw how it was damaging the reputation of someone else she despised, in the very same way.

It is human nature to project our own shortcomings onto others because we don't want to own the fact that there is a part in us that we see in the other person. This is referred to as projection and is a defense mechanism. It might be wise to note that the louder someone screams about what they dislike in others is really just a reflection of what is probably going on in them. Whether it be arrogance, mistrust, or irresponsibility, it could be a good indicator of the underlying dis-ease.

These are difficult conversations, they can be painful, and yet they can be pivotal in moving to long-term solutions. The longer you wait to have the real conversation, the deeper the dis-ease gets embed-

CHAPTER 13

ded in a person's beliefs and behaviors. You need to be able to identify the core issue and not just dabble on the surface.

A Few Possibilities:

- A person who blames others for their failures. Possible dis-ease: Lack of accountability, ownership, or disengagement.
- A leader who doesn't delegate. Possible dis-ease: Control issues, micromanaging, or inability to trust.
- An employee who grandstands or always has to comment regardless of the topic. Possible dis-ease: Lack of self-awareness, lack of self-regulation, self-centered, low self-esteem.
- A leader who allows poor behavior to exist on their team and sweeps it under the carpet, or diminishes the impact on the rest of their team. Possible dis-ease: Conflict avoidance, lacking coaching skills, would rather be liked than lead.
- A leader who moves from one superhero employee to the next, discarding each of them after they fail to meet all of his expectations. Possible dis-ease: Low level of self-awareness, inability to develop talent, unrealistic expectations of others.
- A leader who always has a better idea. Possible dis-ease: Control issues, inability to trust, lack of self-awareness.

These are just a few possibilities and by no means the end-all answers. That is why it is important to ask the questions to get to the real issue and help others see the cost of their behaviors. It is important that we remember to help whomever we are coaching see:

1. How what they are doing is probably giving them the exact opposite results of what they think they are getting.
2. What their behavior is costing them and the cost of not acting, changing, or altering their actions.

(We will also discuss this idea of cost in more detail when we look at the Influencing Model in Chapter 17.)

Accountability and Pushback

When you decide to hold people accountable and help them take ownership for themselves and their work, chances are you going to be met with resistance.

These types of coaching conversations are typically avoided for the very reason that they can be messy and difficult. Instead of dealing with the person and the issue, it may appear that the better choice is to just let sleeping dogs lie. The only problem is that sleeping dogs eventually wake up and can wreak havoc all over the kennel. One of the reasons these conversations get derailed is because the coach is met with a battery of obstacles, otherwise known as defense mechanisms.

These defense mechanisms prevent the coach from getting to the core issues or dis-ease. We refer to this as pushback and it can show up in a number of different ways—whether it is simply failing to respond, raising their voice, walking out, or simply shutting down, all of these defense mechanisms are a form of pushback that create smoke screens to avoid the real issue.

Deflection / Redirection—Redirecting the conversation, pointing a finger away from themselves and toward other people or causes. Pointing at anything other than themselves to push the responsibility away from them. It may also show up by not answering a direct question and redirecting it to another subject or place.

Confusion / Dumbing Down—Responding with phrases like "I don't know" "I have no clue" and "Beats me," are all a forms of dumbing down. Some folks know that if they get emotional or start crying that they can avoid confronting the real issue. Some leaders are very uncomfortable when the person they are coaching begins to cry. Please note that there are times when emotional events happen in all of our lives. I am talking here about the person who starts crying at the drop of a hat when the topic of lateness or failure to deliver results on time comes up, and may even walk out to avoid having the discussion.

The Dragon — Getting angry, combative, or storming out in a huff, while it looks dramatic, is typically just another defense mechanism to avoid dealing with the issue. If I can get away with storming out to avoid the real issue, I will. The tricky part here is that as you get closer to the real issue, the chances are the more dramatic or more intense the anger will be. These behaviors are totally unacceptable and need to be addressed immediately. The longer you wait to address the dragon, the more acceptable or normal it appears to be. It can become a vicious cycle, especially if you are intending to have a conversation with the person about their inability to self-regulate their emotions.

Faux Agreement / Shut Down — Some people will simply shut down. They may do it by not responding at all or they may just start agreeing and saying whatever it is they think you want to hear. They may agree to something simply to get out because the situation is so uncomfortable for them.

The fact is, you are more than likely going to encounter some type of pushback, and you have to be prepared and be crystal clear about three things:

1. **The Why** — Why are you having the conversation in the first place? This needs to be stated in the beginning of the session. "I would like to have a conversation about some of the challenges you are having with meeting deadlines, showing up when you need to be here, your ability to work with others, etc." Without this you can get easily off course.

2. **The Results** — What is the outcome you need to have happen? This should be a little more general in nature because you're not exactly sure what is going to unfold, and when you speak in generalities with an overall spirit of improvement it is less

ACCOUNTABILITY, PUSHBACK, & CURING THE DIS-EASE

threatening. For example: "My hope is that we can come to some agreement about how you can improve your performance in this area."

3. **Awareness** — Awareness in three areas:

   a. **Self-Awareness** — Where do you get stuck, what are your triggers, and where do you need to pay special attention so as not to get derailed? For example, do you typically lay back if they are in agreement, are you fearful of conflict, or do you have a propensity to back off if they push back, or diminish your intention if things get uncomfortable?

   b. **Other-Awareness** — How have conversations with this person gone in the past? Do they have a particular defense mechanism they default to? What is their personality type, communication style, hot buttons, or triggers?

   c. **Plan-Awareness** — This is just a matter of running through the obstacles you have or know that you might run into. If the person starts crying and walks out here is how I will address it and here is what I will say. If they don't answer my question, I will sit and wait for them to answer first before I open my mouth.

One of the best ways to prepare for a tough coaching conversation is to role-play. You may want to grab a peer that you trust and run through a few scenarios with them. Be sure you tell them what you need and how you want them to show up so you have the best chance of running through this as close to the real thing as possible.

Throughout the *The Art of Leading, Coaching, & Influencing Others*™ Leadership Development Program, and as a part of the program, participants work with an accountability partner throughout the program for this specific purpose, as well as a few other reasons. This offers another perspective and allows participants to do a run-through that will make it easier to have the actual conversation.

CHAPTER 13

I cannot emphasize enough the importance of having a trusted peer to work with on these types of issues. The value of getting another perspective on things is worth its weight in antimatter. Yes, antimatter costs $62.5 trillion per gram, gold is only $56 per gram...you get my point.

How to Place Accountability Where It Belongs

As we have discussed in previous sections of this book, you, the coach, need to be vigilant throughout the conversation to be sure the ownership, impact, work, actions, results, and change are where they belong.

Here is a list of possible responses that you can use if and when you encounter any of the defense mechanisms (notice they are all questions):

1. I understand that you would like to talk about Bob, however, I thought we were having a conversation about you and your job?

2. Have you noticed that when I asked what you could do differently, you started talking about Bob? Why is that?

3. I'm sorry but I don't think I asked what you thought others were doing incorrectly, I was asking what it was that you could be doing differently to make things better?

4. If you were to take 100% responsibility for this part of your job, what would you need to do differently?

5. I know this is a tough discussion for you, and I am not okay with you walking out each time we try to come up with a resolution to this issue. What could you change in order to move forward?

6. I am sorry this is so difficult, and we still need to come up with a solution to the problem. That said, what can you do differently going forward?

7. I'm sorry but I believe the question I asked was: "How would you answer that question?" (This is great if you asked a question and they redirect away from answering it).

138

ACCOUNTABILITY, PUSHBACK, & CURING THE DIS-EASE

8. Actually, I think the question I asked only has two possible responses. Yes or No? Which are you choosing?
9. So if you did know how to answer this...what would you say?
10. I'm wondering...if we just brainstormed a few possibilities (answers, solutions, ideas, actions you could take, etc.) what would you say?

I cannot stress enough the importance of using a calm, measured, tentative and nonjudgmental tone. You can implement any of the above questions in a monotone or combative tone. They will be more likely to shut down or push back if the person feels you forcing the conversation. You can and need to deliver these powerful questions with a curious, tentative, artful tone so you can get them to open up, engage, and move toward a solution.

This is why you have to be crystal clear about the intention and the why discussed in the previous section. If it is your intention to control or punish (see the Power vs. Force section in Chapter 2), you are going to be unsuccessful in generating an open dialogue. The other person will sense this display of force and you will get an equal display of force in return.

It requires the skill and craftsmanship to know when, how, and what to say or do in any given situation to help another reach their potential.

In his book *Outliers,* Malcolm Gladwell wrote that "ten thousand hours is the magic number to greatness." And while the theory has been somewhat debunked, I believe his basic premise is correct: you must continue to hone your skills and work on your craft tirelessly because like all great arts, being a great coach takes time.

CHAPTER 14

THE COACHING MINDSET

To Be...or Not to Be

By now I hope you have come to the conclusion on your own that coaching is not something you do. It is not an action you take. It is actually a way of leading; it is a way of *being a leader*. If you understand the theory and concepts behind what coaching is meant to do, then it is much easier to grasp the actual skills needed to be an excellent coach, and an extraordinary leader.

When you do understand the why, you can focus on it and the hows and the whats will fall into place more easily than if you don't have the clarity to focus your energy and are trying to coach and follow a script.

During one of our Leadership Development Programs, we were in the middle of one of the role-playing exercises in which the leaders get an opportunity to really work through a difficult coaching situation they are having with one of their employees. One of the leaders, Robert, was working so hard to exactly follow the Coaching Skills handout because he wanted to it do it "right" the first time.

Robert was more of an analytical person, and so things needed to be in order and there had to be a process to follow, kind of like a coaching-by-numbers system. His role play was awkward and filled with all sorts of starts and stops as he struggled to say *exactly* the right words. He was asking very pointed questions that could easily be answered yes or no, and the other person in the role play was responding to the coaching the exact same way. When I looked around the room, the other people who were observing in order to give feedback were bored and disengaged. They were responding in a similar manner.

Robert would ask a question and head down a particular path. When the person didn't respond the way he expected them to, he got stuck as he searched for the correct word. The other person in the role play sensed this and really pushed Robert in a number of directions. Each time the person Robert was coaching didn't respond according to the guideline, he would get flustered, shake his head, look up at me and say, "I'm stuck again!"

We decided to take a break, and when the other people left the room I pulled him aside and simply asked, "So what's going on up there?" He shared that he wanted to do it right and that he was working way too hard to come up with the perfect words. During the discussion I continued to ask him coaching questions. So where is your focus? What's not working? What do you think needs to shift or change? He decided that he needed to relax because there isn't a perfect way to coach, and that he needed to remind himself why he was having the conversation in the first place.

After the break, Robert went back into the role play with what seemed like a whole new perspective. He sat back, he asked questions, he was curious to understand the thoughts and ideas behind the answers that the other person was giving him, and the whole dynamic shifted. He was having a real, live, genuine coaching conversation. The focus was on the other person answering, not Robert being right!

Afterward, I asked him what that was like. "It was easy!" he said, as his face was plastered with a giant smile. "I just relaxed and asked questions and they did all the work!" Exactly!

Coaching is a way of being: a way of being a leader, not *doing* leadership. I believe there is a stark difference between trying to control or manage a person's behaviors and truly understanding what is going on in their mind. It's about being transparent in your communication, trusting others, and making sure that the accountability, ownership, and impact of the work is on your people, not you. Yes, it is everything we focused on in the Power vs. Force Model, on the Power side, that is. This method will take a little more time initially, but it's either pay me a little now, or pay me big-time later. When you make the decision to spend the majority of your time leading from the Power side of the equation, that's when you really start being effective as a coach!

Short-Term Cost vs. Long-Term Return

Coaching others, asking questions, and being other-focused requires a mindset change. It will require a great deal of time upfront in the beginning as you start to incorporate these new skills into your daily routine and conversations.

I'm not naive to believe that asking questions and waiting for answers from your team members is going to take less time. In fact, you may find that some people love to talk and would spend their entire day in your office chatting away. You will also find the folks that don't dare say a word, they just sit there shrugging their shoulders, saying: "I don't know."

You have to realize that your people are accustomed to interacting with you in a particular way; you have conditioned each of them over time to know what to expect. And now that you're changing the way you interact with them, they will be trying to figure out what happened and if this is a temporary change or something that is going to be permanent. Some of your team members will love the opportunity to answer questions and others are going to be in shock, so give them some time to adjust to this shift in your leadership style.

You will probably have a few awkward conversations. You may even find yourself wishing that you never even attempted any of this soft skills coaching "crap!"

You didn't acquire your leadership habits overnight, and they aren't going to change overnight. You just need to be consistent. Most importantly, you need to make sure you aren't beating yourself up for not getting this perfect. There is no perfect, and if you attempt to be perfect, you will be sorely disappointed.

When you do have a coaching conversation that doesn't go well it actually creates an extraordinary opportunity. Here's how:

It gives you the opportunity to go back to that person and own the fact that the conversation didn't go the way you intended. You can tell the other person what your intention was, and then ask them how they experienced the conversation. After they reply, ask them what would have made it a better conversation and then see where that takes you.

When you do this, five things can happen:

1. They will have much more respect for you because you owned that you messed up.

2. It can be an even more powerful conversation than the first could have been, because in owning the truth, you have made yourself vulnerable and vulnerability builds trust! Yes, vulnerability builds trust because it sends the message that you are a human being and you're not perfect.

3. By taking these actions you are teaching them how great leaders lead; you are teaching them that it is safe to own their mistakes and, therefore, in a sense, you give the other person permission to do the same.

4. You show them that no matter your title or position, you have to continue to learn new skills and try new things.

5. You will feel better about the conversation and you will stop playing it over and over in your head while you beat yourself up internally.

The Ultimate Goal of Coaching

The ultimate goal of coaching is perfectly aligned with the ultimate goal of leading. It is to focus your energy and attention on others. Ask them great questions so that you can light the path in front of them, which can be strewn with obstacles that they can't or won't see. It is

THE COACHING MINDSET

also about shining the light on their strengths, their brilliance, and their genius, so that they can engage their best selves in their work. And in doing this, the results and the productivity of your team and others around you will grow exponentially.

CHAPTER 15

COACHING: 10 THINGS TO REMEMBER, 10 THINGS TO FORGET, 10 THINGS TO DO

Achieving extraordinary results never happens when you sit back and wait for it to arrive on your doorstep one day. If you truly want to achieve extraordinary results, you have to be willing to do whatever it takes to move yourself forward. No one is going to do it for you. There are things you will need to remember, things that you will have to unlearn or forget, and there are things that you will need to start doing. I have summarized the most important takeaways from this chapter in a format that guides you through making the transition from managing to becoming a coach. After a while, after you have gone through the period where you have to focus and be intentional about integrating these actions into your daily routine, there will be a shift. You will shift from having to work at them and consciously choose, to becoming unconscious and not thinking about it. Why? Because they will be so engrained into how you have embodied becoming a leader. And that is when you will have truly changed.

10 Things to Remember

1. Remember that coaching is all about the person you are coaching first and foremost.

2. Each person is different. They are not you and don't think like you. They aren't just like the last person you coached, so don't treat them like they are. Each person is unique.

3. Remember that questions will help you to see others' perspectives more clearly, and only by understanding their perspective can you effectively coach anyone.

4. Questioning others takes time; it is truly an art, and, therefore, you cannot rush the process.

5. Fear can block others from moving forward; your job as a coach is to help them see that they are stopping themselves (and where), and help them find a path forward.

6. The greater the fear, the bigger the gremlin; the bigger the gremlin, the more resistance you will get.

7. Being a victim is about playing small. Coaching others to create choices will empower them to move forward and stop playing small.

8. Remember to coach to the core of the issue and get to the underlying beliefs. Coaching the behaviors is like treating the symptoms and not the dis-ease.

9. Your job as a coach is to make sure the accountability, ownership, and impact is in the hands of the employee—not on you the coach.

10. The long-term, sustainable solution to coaching people is to make sure you take the long-term approach to influencing them by helping them find their own solutions to their problems.

10 Things to Forget

1. Forget the idea that you are responsible *for* the people you lead; you are responsible *to* them, to create an environment where they can be successful—if they choose to be.

2. Forget the idea that you can control anything or anyone other than your own thoughts.

3. Forget the idea that you can fool anyone. People see and sense when someone is being inauthentic. If you're not authentic, it is just a matter of time until the truth reveals itself.

4. Forget thinking that if you just keep telling people what to do or how to change that they will actually change. You're not that powerful!

5. Forget the idea that being a leader who coaches others entitles you to anything other than an opportunity to influence others *to do or to be their best.*

6. Forget thinking that because you are a leader who coaches that you can stop learning and developing your own skills.

7. Forget the idea that the skills and methods that made you successful as an individual contributor, will automatically make you a great coach.

8. Forget the idea that coaching is something you do or a set of actions you take rather than a way of leading or a way of *being* a leader.

9. Forget the idea that shortcuts exist on the path to becoming a great coach. It takes effort, energy, and focus!

10. Forget all the old beliefs that tell you you're not enough, that you won't succeed, and if you make a mistake that you're doomed for the rest of your life.

10 Things to Do

1. Start your next conversation with one of your direct reports with the following questions:
   a. How are things going?
   b. What's working really well in your job right now?
   c. What's not?
      i. What are you doing to work on the stuff that's not?
      ii. How can I support you?
      iii. When can we touch base so I can hear how you're progressing?

CHAPTER 15

2. Start observing your propensity to tell others your opinion, how to do things, or your experience, rather than how often and how consistently you ask great questions.

3. Instead of judging yourself as good or bad, start noticing what you're skilled at and what you're not. Then start looking for ways to improve in the unskilled areas.

4. When you slip up or backslide, step back and look at the situation from an observer's perspective. Think to yourself: "Isn't that interesting I started to get frustrated when I felt that they weren't listening or hearing me!"

5. Make a list of three or four things that your direct reports do extremely well, and share one per week with each of them over the course of the next few weeks.

6. Start making a list of two or three people who work for you that have the potential to replace you.

7. Have a conversation with each of them, by asking questions and discovering what they believe is the next step in their career, and begin developing them as leaders.

8. Make a list of 10 go-to questions that will open, continue, and sustain a coaching conversation (What's working about...? What's not working about...? Can you say more about that...? You get the picture). These will become your "go-to" list and need to be imprinted in your beliefs.

9. Start incorporating those 10 questions into your daily conversations.

10. After three months of consistently practicing these skills, share this book with your leaders, so they can follow in your path.

Practicing the Art
Ribbon On Your Finger

Over the course of the next three weeks, review these lists at the beginning and end of the week as a checklist to see how you are progressing. The first week focus on the 10 Things to Remember, the second week focus on the 10 Things to Forget, and the third week, focus on the 10 Things to Do. Use each category and turn them into a checklist. For example: "Did I forget that?" "Do I remember?" "Do I..." You get the picture.

PART III
MASTERING THE ART OF INFLUENCING OTHERS

CHAPTER 16
INFLUENCE VS. MANIPULATION

Every single day you have to make a decision that determines whether or not what you are reading, hearing, and seeing is the truth, a twisted version of the truth, or a complete and utter distortion.

The emergence of social media and the ability to put anything you want online has exponentially increased the swiftness of delivery as well as the breadth to what we now have labeled as "fake news."

It has become so prolific that we now have people with cell phones staging fake events and then plastering them on Facebook for the sole purpose of gaining attention and manipulating the audience to believe something that is not true. On the other extreme, it has also revealed the darkest side of humanity.

On April 16, 2017, a man posted a video asking an innocent elderly man walking down the street to say a women's name. He then shot the elderly 74-year-old Robert Godwin Sr. for no reason at all. This video sat on Facebook for nearly two hours. It gets worse. Scammers started GoFundMe pages to raise money for the family. It turns out that none of them were genuine, they were simply sick people, taking advantage of a tragedy.

CHAPTER 16

Some people consider it art. For example, Paul Horner, labeled by the Huffington Post as a "performance artist" and by the Washington post as "The Internet's most prolific hoax artist" makes a living off of writing fake news, scamming folks, and then blames the fact that people believed him on their stupidity. It is the ultimate in self-centered, self-obsessed narcissism. When you dig a little deeper, you will typically find a personal agenda, like he hates Donald Trump, probably because he thinks Trump is a narcissist.

It doesn't matter whether you like Donald Trump or not, what matters is that people like Paul Horner purposely try to deceive others to push their agenda, to manipulate you, create turmoil, inflict damage, and then point the finger of blame at their victims.

So, what does this have to do with leadership? A lot. Leaders are people who influence others to do or to be their best. What do you call it when a person is solely focused on bringing out the worst in others? A manipulator.

Trust is the cornerstone of leadership; without it people will simply not follow you. If you are a leader, and you turn around and nobody is behind you, you are probably not leading anyone. If you have the privilege and opportunity to lead others, you have to be crystal clear on the difference between being a leader and being a manipulator. Leading is an art, manipulation is anything *but* art.

We discussed early on the difference between manipulation and influence. We've spent the last fifteen chapters talking about leadership and coaching, and now we're going to delve deeper into the concept of influence and share a model or framework to which you can apply influence in almost every situation. This chapter is designed to briefly review how we define influence, and then talk about two different approaches, one that works most of the time and one that doesn't work nearly as often in the context of true leadership.

156

Remember...It's All About the Intention

Let's quickly revisit Webster's definition of influence:

"The power to change or affect someone or something: the power to cause changes without directly forcing them to happen. A person or thing that affects someone or something in an important way."

By now, you understand the importance of asking questions when it comes to the Art of Coaching. And, while not every conversation is a coaching conversation, when it comes to helping others see a different perspective, your role as a coach is critical in helping others to see things in a different light so they can make a more informed decision as to whether or not they want to change.

As mentioned early in the book, the difference between manipulation and influence is about the intention of the person who is attempting to influence others. Recall that manipulation is about being self-centered, while influence is about being other-centered and focusing on what the other person needs first. When you are asking questions, you are attempting to understand the views and opinions of the other person and that process is about being other-centered.

There is a fine line between influence and manipulation based on our description of whether a person is being self-centered or other-centered. I have worked with folks who have embraced the whole idea of asking questions, but then turn the process around in a way that is forcing people toward a particular outcome. When this happens, that line is being crossed.

You can argue back and forth about what is influence and what is manipulation. You can even try to come up with a legalistic approach and attempt to define it so clearly that there is no room open to interpretation—similar to the way society tries to write laws that address what is politically correct and what isn't. It is impossible.

There is the law, and there is the spirit of the law. You can set laws so that people obey its literal interpretation; I don't think you can write

CHAPTER 16

a law that can govern a person's intent. Only the person themselves can ever know what their intention truly is.

One person's influence is another person's manipulation. Therefore, I prefer to leave it up to the individual leader to decide whether they are influencing, or they are attempting to manipulate. Besides, the truth is that you are the only one who knows your true intention. I trust you'll make the right choices and when you don't...you will realign, readjust, and make it right.

Crossing the Line

I find that when a leader is bumping up against these three obstacles, they shift easily from a place of influence and toward manipulation. While it may be one or the other, most of the time it is combination of a little bit of all three:

- **Impatience** — I am too busy to want or need to understand what you think; I want to stop wasting time and dancing around the real issue by asking a bunch of questions.
- **Control** — I am the boss and what I say goes; when you become the boss then you can make the rules, do what you want; besides it is my decision anyway.
- **Ego** — I don't care what you think. I care what I think and what I want and what I think is...I already have an agenda for what you need to say and do, so just do it and we'll be fine.

These thoughts happen every day in the workplace; the fallacy is that we believe most leaders would flat out deny any of the above, and yet I see them playing out with my coaching clients and the attendees of our programs.

You can't fake your intention. Whether your leadership base is self-centered or other-centered, it always comes out in the end. It doesn't matter how nice you wrap up your intention, or what eloquently spoken words you use, people see through it.

158

Influencing: Outside-In

Your greatest ability to influence others comes from the fact that influencing others is an inside-out job! Before I explain why, answer the following questions honestly:

1. In a conversation with another person, do you spend more time sharing your thoughts and ideas, or listening to theirs?

2. In a conversation where you are trying to get your point across or get someone to buy in to your idea, do you typically start by sharing your thoughts, ideas, opinions, or needs before you understand the other person and their opinion about the topic?

Can I let you in on a little secret?

Until you know what the other person thinks, believes, or feels about a particular topic or situation...your opinion doesn't mean anything when it comes to influencing others!

Most leaders feel that the way to get their point across is to first tell the other person what they are thinking, what they want, and sometimes even how they want it done. They feel that the more words they use to tell them what they want, the more effectively they are influencing others.

I have observed plenty of situations in which leaders spend inordinate amounts of time and energy approaching others from the outside-in. This requires that they tell (make statements) in an attempt to convince others to listen, to follow, to understand, to change, or to take action with very poor results.

Influencing: Inside-Out

Real influencing requires that you take the time to start on the inside of the other person so you can first understand what they think.

Why? Because if you don't know where they stand on a topic, how

CHAPTER 16

do you know if they are already on the same page as you, or whether they're diametrically opposed to your thoughts and ideas? The gap that exists between where the person is and where you are on the topic will determine the path you take to get them to move.

And yes, we all know leaders who feel they are entitled to be obeyed or followed. That doesn't make you a great leader, in fact that makes you an insecure low-level supervisor.

Influencing from the inside-out begins by asking great questions. And, the power of asking great questions is critical whether you are coaching, leading, or facilitating others.

5 Things That Happen When You Influence From the Inside-Out:

- It engages the other person in the conversation that ultimately increases their buy-in.
- It sends the message that their thoughts on the topic are valued — and if their thoughts are valued, *they* are valued. Most people do not feel valued even when you tell them because you have to show them!
- Your probability of successfully influencing goes up dramatically because you know what they think about the topic. If you ask the right questions, you will be better suited to handle their objections and misunderstandings before you share your thoughts on the matter.
- It gives you the opportunity to see how the person thinks, which gives you the opportunity to influence their thought process, and, ultimately, their future behavior.
- Your ability to lead others will dramatically increase because your team members will want to follow you knowing that they have some level of involvement in the conversation. This refers to the locus of control, a critical component that dramatically impacts a person's level of engagement in their work.

At first this may seem counterintuitive because it is diametrically opposed to what most of us have been taught: to focus on ourselves and

160

our own needs first before we understand and focus on others and their needs. However, as you become more adept at asking great questions to draw out the other person's thoughts and opinions, you will get more of what you need more often.

Practicing the Art
Clarifying Intentions

Below is a list of behaviors that would tell you that you are more self-centered than other-centered. How many of these apply to you?

1. Have you ever taken credit for the work your team does in an attempt to make yourself look better?
2. Have you ever placed blame or thrown others under the bus to cover up a mistake you made?
3. You micromanage or allow your leaders to micromanage because of your need to control others, the process, or your reputation.
4. You believe you and you alone can fix the problem because you're so great and you're the only great one who knows how, even when it is a complex issue.
5. Have you ever condemned others for the very behavior you exhibit or have committed in the past?
6. Have you ever intentionally hidden information from a conversation to make the facts appear to be something other than what they really are?
7. Have you on more than three occasions thought that you really don't like being a leader? And you continue in the position because you are not willing to give up the perks or additional compensation?
8. Do you consistently take feedback personally and dismiss it as simply someone else's opinion?

CHAPTER 16

9. Do you consistently respond back to others, "I guess we will just have to agree to disagree," in order to be stubborn, inflexible, or have to be right?
10. Do you feel that you have the ability to change others if they would only listen to you and follow your advice?

So, how did you do? Most of the time people want to know how many yes answers is too many, or what's normal. The truth is you already know the answer to that question. Sometimes we look to others to verify or substantiate whether or not we are normal. We may seek out others who align with our conclusions or results so we can justify our findings or beliefs. You know whether or not you are more self-centered or other-centered; the questions here are to help you get clarification. If I were to give you a low rating, you could still justify your position or you might decide to change.

The good news is that you can decide to change, it just comes down to making a decision about how you want to lead going forward from this moment. Just like the difference between influence and manipulation, it all boils down to your intention.

CHAPTER 17

THE ART OF INFLUENCING MODEL

People don't want to be sold or told what to do or what to think, they want to have the choice to buy in to the thought, the idea, or the action. That is what influence is all about. The concepts and overall thought process in this section are at the heart of influencing others and apply to leading, coaching, and facilitating. It is designed to take you through a step-by-step process. After you have utilized the model and become comfortable with each step, you will realize that not every situation requires each and every step. However, if you follow the basic formula and adjust to the various situations or circumstances, I promise you will see an exponential increase in your ability to influence others more effectively.

Step 1: Defining Where You Want / Need to Be / Do / Go

The first step in the Influencing Model is similar to the first step in most 12-step programs such as Alcoholics Anonymous. It's the only one you have to get absolutely clear. If you don't, the rest of the steps won't work very well. The first step is all about clarity. You have to be crystal clear about what you are trying to accomplish. What is the end result?

CHAPTER 17

- It may be for one of your direct reports to see how they are creating obstacles to their success or the team's success.
- It could be to help someone step up and be more responsible so that they can get the promotion or advance their development.
- It may be to influence the CEO to buy in to one of your ideas and hire more people because you need more people to meet productivity targets.
- It may be to get your team on the same page about a particular topic so they can be a more effective unit instead of individual silos.
- It may even be to get a business partner or internal customer to buy your product regardless of whether it is an IT project, marketing concept, or new data storage tool.

Notice that in the last bullet point I didn't say for you to sell your idea, but for your customer to buy in to your idea. This is a critical difference because studies show that people despise being sold to, but they love to buy. Again, think about what most people say about the car buying process. They hate it, feel pressured, and most transactions feel slimy. That happens because the salesperson is only focused on one thing: getting the sale. It is all about them and not about the customer. I bring this up because if you set up this whole process in and around you, you will get yourself in trouble. And, while I understand that the example is about selling, it is really more about buying. It is about buying in and getting buy-in. That is what influence is about!

Yes, a lack of clarity here at the starting point could be the kiss of death for the rest of the process. It will definitely be dead if you make this all about you!

Step 2: Defining Where You Are Right Now

Once you get clarity on where you're headed with the conversation, you have to take a good look and decide where you currently are in relationship to where you want to be. While this may sound simplistic and obvious, you need to be clear how big the gap is between those two points.

For example, if you want to increase the trust level with one of your direct reports so you can work together more effectively and give them more responsibility (where you want to go), but you have unaddressed issues with them because you are afraid to have tough conversations (where you are), then that determines your path.

That very same situation will be completely different if you have had the challenging conversations with them along the way. Then, you would take a completely different path because the gap between where you are and where you want to go is not as wide. By the way, if you don't have the challenging conversations and avoid them, just assume that the trust level is low. Conversations that hold folks accountable actually build trust. If you are not willing to hold your team members accountable, they won't trust you. Why? Because you send a message when you agree and commit to an action, and when you don't follow up to make sure it is complete, it will make them think that you don't do what you say you're going to do.

Step 3: Understanding Where the Individual is Right Now

The next step is all about determining where the individual you're attempting to influence is in relationship to where the objective is. This is a critical relationship, because their perception of where they are and where they need to end up is the most important factor.

It doesn't matter if their belief or idea is distorted or not what you think it should be, what matters is that you understand what they believe or think about the topic. The wider the gap between where they are in relationship to the topic and where you need them to be is critical for you to understand. If you don't know how wide this gap is, you will be much less effective. For example, if you and your direct report have two diametrically opposed perceptions about the level of

CHAPTER 17

trust between you, that will certainly impact how you approach them. If you assume that the trust level between you is extremely high and they believe it is extremely low, it really doesn't matter what you think because their perception is their reality and that is the starting point where you need to begin the process. Now you can see why your opinion matters far less than theirs.

One way to ask them where they are on such a subjective topic as trust, is to frame it in an objective way that allows them to put a number on their level of trust. A great question to ask them is, "On a scale of 1 to 10, with 1 being low and 10 being high, how would you rate the trust level between us?" If you're thinking 5 and they're thinking 10, you have a gap and that will impact how you proceed. Once rated, you know what they truly think and you can work from there. Then, when you have a good idea of the relationship between these three different points (perspectives) you can move to the next step.

This may be where you start your conversation or coaching session, so it is important that you state the purpose for the conversation. For example, "Chris, I wanted to have a conversation with you about improving our working relationship going forward. It is perfectly fine to keep this objective general and nonjudgmental. If it is a delicate or complex issue around behavior or performance, then you may use something like, "Chris, I wanted to have a conversation about how you might improve your performance in a few key areas." It is general in nature and gives them enough insight into the topic you want to discuss without putting them on the defensive.

Whether you are having a one-on-one coaching conversation, facilitating a group meeting with ten of your team members, or trying to get your CEO to buy into your idea, this process of asking questions is critically important to understanding where they stand on a particular issue or topic. Skip this step and you will struggle immensely.

THE ART OF INFLUENCING MODEL

Step 4: Identify the Desires & the Need

During this step it is important to understand what the other person's needs are and what is important to them. This could be specific to certain parts of their work, a specific situation that is or isn't working for them, or in relation to their career development.

Most of the time we don't ask, we assume that we know what they want or we assume that they want the exact same thing that we do. This is not true, and is especially the case when dealing with different generations. Baby boomers are driven folks; they are the poster children for workaholism, and they live to work, generally speaking. Millennials, on the other hand, were raised at a different time and value different things. Neither of them are wrong nor right, they're just different. If you are a baby boomer and you are working to coach or influence a millennial, for example, you need to understand what they want and what they desire. You do this by asking questions.

A few examples of questions you could ask may include:
- What is it that you want most?
- What would make this an ideal situation?
- If you could make this right, what would need to happen?
- What's the most important thing to you?
- How would things be different if this were to happen?

As you can see, the questions are future-based; they are beyond the current situation and the present moment. You need to know what the other person wants and what is important to them so you can understand what is the underlying motivation, the thing they want, or the outcome they are seeking. Additionally, just because they tell you what it is they want, doesn't mean you are promising to get them there. Some leaders are afraid to have this conversation because they're afraid that if the person voices some outrageous request they have to deliver, so it's best to not discuss it. That's not true. If an employee believes they deserve and want a $20-an-hour raise or to work from home five days a week, then you have the option to say, "I understand what it is that you want, and I know that it is not possible to achieve here at our organization. I'm wondering if another company would be willing to help you meet your need?" Remember that regardless of what they say, think, or believe, if you are unaware of their perspective, you are really at a loss to resolve the situation. It is better to know than to blindly assume you are both on the same page.

Step 5: Identify the Pain & the Cost

Some folks struggle with the idea of creating pain or raising the pain awareness level. However, we're really talking about creating a picture of the costs or the consequences, if the person you're coaching or influencing doesn't get what they want or desire. This is an important relationship because, as you know, with anything in life, there are costs associated with them. T.S. Eliot refers to this in his work titled *Four Quartets*. He refers to this as the Universal Law of Compensation, which says that every action or inaction has a cost associated with it. If we spend time at work to get a project done, it has an associated cost that we can't spend that time anywhere else, so we have to weigh the cost of staying late at work or going home to our spouse or family. We can't have both, even if we can do the work at home. Some generations may not have had to experience consequences for actions or inactions while they were growing up, which makes this an even more important step when working with them.

Identifying the cost is also done by asking questions.

Here are a few examples of questions you might ask at this stage of the conversation:
- What happens if you don't get what you want?
- What's it costing you? The team?
- What's the biggest challenge facing...you, the team, the company, etc.?

THE ART OF INFLUENCING MODEL

- What's not working about this...situation, process, product, project, approach, etc.?
- What happens if you don't succeed?
- What happens if you don't change a thing?

It is critically important that you get the other person to identify the cost or the consequences and that they speak it out loud. You want them to be aware that these are their words and not yours. Chances are, they have heard your words plenty prior to this conversation, especially if it is a recurring situation.

Step 6: Identify the Obstacles

At this point in the conversation you are starting to get the person to realize what is getting in their way of where they want to go (Step 4). In reality, what you are doing is shining a light so they can better see the obstacles that they are placing in their own way. You have to be careful here to make sure that they don't deflect the responsibility on people or places they have no control over or that lead to blaming others.

- What's stopping you from getting what you want?
- What keeps getting in the way of your success, progress, etc.? The team's success, progress, etc.?
- What's keeping you stuck?
- How does staying stuck serve you?
- How does continuing down this path get you the promotion you said you wanted earlier in our conversation?

While the last two questions seem odd, they are two of the most powerful questions listed (and especially the last one) because that is where you are putting the desire and the obstacle right next to each other for them to see the gap between the two. One of two things might happen here:

CHAPTER 17

1. They will have an awakening, see the gap, and realize they need to take action to change it, which will lead you into Step 7.

2. They see the difference and come to the realization that what they say they want is not what they really want, or that they aren't willing to pay the cost it requires to change. Otherwise they wouldn't be doing it, so continue to the next step.

3. They may need a few more questions to help them understand why they are choosing to stay stuck or in the place they currently are, so dig a little deeper by asking questions to help them gain more clarity.

Most folks will deny that doing something such as playing small, being late, not pulling their weight, or not engaging with other team members, for example, is serving them in any way. You will find that if you stay with the questions, playing small may turn into not wanting to fail, or being wrong in public, or another reason that keeps them safe. (Refer to Chapter 4 for more on this.)

Step 7: Identify The Actions Needed to Change / Move / Grow

This step moves the person into taking action. As in coaching, you may get some pushback (refer to Chapter 4, Gremlins & Fear F.I.L.L.E.R.S.™). This step is where you gain clarity on possible solutions. It is important to remember that these are not your ideas that you have already thought through for the person. These need to be their solutions, as it will create a deeper sense of buy-in and commitment. Some leaders can't help themselves, so they may attempt to offer solutions here because it may feel like a more efficient use of their time—especially if they already are feeling like they have spent enough time on this conversation.

While that may be true, it is not the most effective path. Chances are you have offered them solutions in the previous twelve conversations you've had about the same topic. Also, if this is a non-coaching

170

conversation with a peer or client, you want them to lead with the actions they believe are the next right step. This will give them more of a sense of control and buy-in to the plan or idea because they are their ideas and solutions. This is critical; you want them choosing to buy in and not to feel as if they are being sold to.

Here is a list of some questions that can help you move from discussing and into action:
- So what needs to happen here (next)?
- If you were to take one step forward, what would it be?
- What's the next step you'd be willing to take to achieve the results you want?
- What actions could (will) you take to move forward, achieve your goals, the team's goals, etc.?
- What do you need to do between now and the next time we meet?
- If you were going to plan for the next step after that, what would it be?
- And the next?

Action is the tipping point that gets the person moving forward and beginning to move past their self-imposed obstacles. If you do a great job of creating a number of options they could choose to take, they will have a greater sense of empowerment when you ask them to decide on the top two or three. Once you have those nailed down you are ready to go to the next step, which is all about getting agreement, commitment, and holding them accountable.

Step 8: Get Agreement, Commitment, & Hold Accountable

A number of leaders will stop once they get a few ideas on the table because they will feel that they got commitment and everybody can move forward. However, if you want to increase the likelihood of being successful here, you need to be as specific as possible and be sure that you are both crystal clear about what they are committing to doing. Obviously, if this is a client or peer, it may be a little less about accountability and more about the agreement. It starts with agreeing to the actions or decisions. Based on the previous step, if they came up with five great ideas, you may want to narrow it down to two or three.

Here are a few questions to ask in a few different situations:
- So that we're on the same page...you're committing to...is that right?
- What I've heard so far, is that you are willing to do x if I am willing to do y? Did I get that right?
- So that we're in agreement...you agreed to...?
- So you've decided on option 1 and option 3, as long as I can get you the project completed by the first of the month? Is that correct?
- What should we do if your plan isn't getting you the results that you want? How do you want to handle things then?
- How do you want to handle things if you get off track? How will we know you're off track?
- How can I support you? What would that look like?

Notice that the fifth and sixth bulleted points are geared for a one-on-one coaching conversation, particularly when you've had the conversation before and it has not gone well. It is a way to let the person come up with a new suggestion in case they get off track. Remember, they have to come up with the action, the consequence, or the way to get back on track. It is critically important that you have this conversation early on and at this step instead of waiting for the person to fall off track and then have to have yet another conversation about the same topic.

Be sure to pay attention to the very last bulleted point in which the leader asks how they can support the other party. One of the mistakes a leader who is having a coaching conversation will make is that they offer support up front prior to letting the other person come up

THE ART OF INFLUENCING MODEL

with actions and committing to them. When you do that, you are taking away the opportunity to let your employee work through and think through the issue. I have noticed in role-playing that because it may be uncomfortable for some leaders to get agreement, commitment, and create consequences, they try to soften the conversation by coming across as helpful. Don't diminish the effectiveness of the conversation or take away from your employee's ability to solve their own issues or work their way out of a challenging situation. You may feel better in the short-term, but you are sacrificing the long-term changes in behavior that will grow and develop your employee in a much bigger way.

I cannot emphasize enough the importance of this step, because it is where you put the road plan in place and determine if you have a good course for reaching your destination. The true test is determined in the next step, however, if you get this one wrong you're almost assured of failing on the next step, which is where the rubber actually meets the road.

Step 9: Praise / Coach / Thank / Move On

If both parties do what is agreed upon, then you have influenced them successfully, and if that is the case then you can heap praise upon them and yourself. Unfortunately, as easy as it is to do, it is one of the most under-utilized forms of positive reinforcement and motivation in the workplace today.

Praising your people for the positive changes in behaviors or for accomplishments is a core need in all of us. Research shows that these feelings are genetically encoded in our DNA. *Harvard Business Review* published an article in June of 2014 that discussed the neurochemistry of positive conversations. The article goes into some detail about the chemical impact of positive and negative conversations and the relationship to the neurochemicals oxytocin and cortisol.

When we are successful (in different ways), our bodies release different chemicals into our blood systems and those drugs make us feel

173

CHAPTER 17

good. Simon Sinek's book, *Leaders Eat Last: Why Some Teams Pull Together and Others Don't,* is probably one of the more easily readable and comprehensive books I have read on the topic.

Leaders have a tendency to either overpraise or underpraise; the unfortunate reality is that most underpraise. There are countless studies on the negative impact that a lack of recognition or praise has on your team and how this lack of recognition negatively impacts the bottom line. Giving others praise is the most cost-effective motivator of people and yet so many leaders don't seem to get this aspect of leadership quite right. A survey conducted by the White Water Strategy group indicated that being praised can have the same impact on job satisfaction as a very small increase in compensation.

If the situation was one in which you were attempting to influence a peer, a client, or your manager, praise is still required and can be executed with a simple "Thank you!" But as with all good praise, it needs to be as specific as possible and include: a specific action, to a specific person, about something that is specific to them and what they did. "Hey nice job!" just doesn't cut it and can be seen in an unappreciative or disingenuous way.

One of the most influential and authentic ways to give praise is to be as specific as possible. Giving feedback to a specific person about something they did specifically speaks to their strengths or talents as an individual.

For example:

"Susan, I really liked the way you spoke out in the meeting and shared your insights on the integration project. I think it really emphasizes your ability to explain complex problems in a way that everyone in the room could understand. Great job!"

Rather than:

"Susan, nice job in the integration project meeting."

In the event you don't have success, then you have a few options. If it is in a one-on-one situation with a direct report, you may have to have a follow-up coaching session with them and address why the situation didn't work out and intensify the consequences.

If it is with a peer and you can't work through the issue, then it may be time to take it to the next level and get a little different perspective. Sometimes we are so engrossed in an issue we may be blinded from seeing it as clearly as we need to in order to move to a solution. If the other party is equally blinded, a third party may help the both of you break though and create some new options for each of you.

Things don't always go the way you want them to, so at times, depending on the situation, you have to let go and move on. For example, if it's situation in which you are attempting to get buy-in from a customer or business partner on a new IT program, you can review the situation and see if there is a reason they're still not buying in; otherwise, sometimes you just have to cut your losses and move on.

One of the greatest lessons I learned over the course of my career was when to let go of a prospect, a customer, an employee, and even a marriage. That occurred when I realized it wasn't the right deal for me, them, or the both of us. As a leader, knowing when a problem employee needs to go is as important as knowing which one to hire.

Most leaders hold onto to problem children way too long. If you work through the Coaching & Influencing Models in this book and you're still having issues, you may have to change your target and work to move them out.

The Journey of Influence

T.S. Eliot once said: "We shall not cease from exploration, and the end of all our exploring will be to arrive where we started and know the place for the first time."

I find that if you approach influencing with a curious mindset, and if you ask great questions so that you can truly understand the other person's perspective without having it clouded by your wants, needs, desires, and beliefs, then this process is indeed an exploration.

After you have worked through all the steps, you should end up back at Step 1, however, you will be arriving at the place you started and knowing it in a completely different way. You will know it and see it through the eyes of the person you are influencing. In doing so, they will guide you through each and every step, which will lead you to where you wanted to or needed to be, to do, or to go.

Practicing the Art
What Have You Noticed About Others' Ability to Influence?

1. Make a list of the people who report directly to you.
2. Rate each person on a scale of 1 to 10 (with 1 being low and 10 being high) in regard to their ability to influence others.
3. Write down what you believe would increase their Influence Quotient by +1 and +2.
4. Have a conversation with each person to assess their rating on how well they think they influence others.
5. Compare the ratings and create a strategy to move them into action using the Influencing Model you learned in this chapter.

CHAPTER 18

THE ART OF FACILITATION

Meetings are typically the go-to way of getting a group of people together to resolve issues and most of them are a boring waste of time.

Facilitation, however, is a style of meeting that increases the level of influence of a leader exponentially because it is extremely empowering. Just like with coaching, facilitating is a process that gives the people the freedom to realize that they have the answers to their challenges within themselves. When you facilitate the group you are leveraging the combined power of all of the individuals to find their own solutions.

Coaching on Steroids

When you coach, you are typically working in a one-on-one situation. Your focus and attention are on the individual you are coaching. When you are facilitating a group, your focus needs to be the entire group and the focus on the wants and needs of the individual needs to be woven into an overall group purpose and objective.

For some people, the very idea of standing in front of a group of people and speaking is horrifying. Yes, we've all heard that public speaking is one of the greatest fears known to mankind, and yet, your ability to stand in front of a group and get them to collaborate so that they can produce results is at the core of what Emotional Intelligence (EQ) is all about. This is why, as a leader, working on and developing your EQ is critically important. Facilitating magnifies this concept tenfold.

In coaching you have to be really great at asking questions and letting the person that you're coaching find their own answers.

Facilitating is no different, it is about facilitating a rich and robust conversation within a group of people who are focused on achieving one goal or purpose.

Whether that goal is to brainstorm ideas, problem-solve, find solutions, get group buy-in or consensus, make decisions, affect change, etc., your role is to take yourself out of the center of these conversations, step aside, and allow the group members to shine.

The power of facilitating a group conversation comes from the fact that you are basically taking the power of a single coaching conversation and multiplying it by ten. That can happen if you are willing to take yourself out of the limelight, get past any old self-limiting beliefs about presenting, and put aside your ego and your need to be the center of attention. Most importantly, just like in leading and coaching, the facilitation process is not about you, it's about the group.

Having a conversation with ten people rather than one is obviously more efficient. When you trust the group to find the answers, you are leveraging the collective knowledge and experience of the entire group, which is an extremely powerful way to solve problems or create solutions.

The problem with most meetings is that they don't leverage the power of the people in the room. Why wouldn't you take advantage of having more people, with more ideas, who can answer more questions, and create more solutions than any one person ever could?

And yet, one of the biggest obstacles to a successful facilitation process is the leader. Most leaders don't like giving up control of *their* meeting. They may feel that they need to be in the center driving the

THE ART OF FACILITATION

group toward a solution. This is true especially if a leader comes to a meeting already having decided what to do, how to do it, and is just going through the motions of faking a discussion to give the team a false sense of ownership.

If you understand the basic premise of coaching, you can facilitate a great process or meeting, and it will be even easier and require less effort than you ever thought possible. Second, once you learn to effectively facilitate a meeting, you will learn that if you trust the process no matter what is unfolding in the meeting, you will always know how to effectively overcome any issue or handle any situation. In fact, you will realize that you have more resources and more options available to you so that any thoughts of being stuck and not knowing what to do will completely disappear.

It's as Easy as 1-2-3

As with all interactions that you are preparing for, whether a conversation, a coaching conversation, a meeting, or a presentation, the most important step is to ask yourself: Why? Why am I having this conversation? Why am I having this meeting? Remember without the why, the how and the what don't matter. You would be surprised at the lack of clarity most leaders have when calling a meeting together, the purpose is either so vague that no one is clear why they are there, or it is so big that they cannot possibly accomplish the task in the allotted time. Either way they cannot achieve success.

So the question becomes: why do I want to have this meeting? It could be for any number of reasons, but for the sake of example, let's just say that your team is struggling with a new process for designing and delivering software to your client. Let's call the old process waterfall and the new process agile. This is actually a real situation and a transformation that has been happening in the world of Information Technology for quite some time. However, for some folks this is a big shift because it is complex and a major shift in the approach to

179

CHAPTER 18

collaborating amongst the team and the customer. What makes it even more challenging is that typically, analytical people are usually pretty risk adverse; they are driven by a need to be right, and being wrong, especially in public, is a big fear. I chose this topic as an example, because *it is* complex and I want to demonstrate the simplicity of a conversation that needs to happen. So let me give you a little background in very simplistic terms.

Waterfall was the old way of designing and delivering software to a client where the design team got all of the requirements upfront and then built the program and delivered the product. Sometimes the end product wasn't quite right because over time the client's needs shifted and they didn't communicate, or other variables came into play and the project got delayed. Sometimes a project got delivered that didn't meet the requirements of the client and so a lot of time and energy was wasted on a product that didn't work or meet the customer's needs. So the team had to go back to square one.

Agile is the newer method, where you build as you go, you work together more closely with the client, and check in every two weeks or so on your progress. For a lot of IT people, who are accustomed to delivering the finished product at the end, this is a huge leap. Agile requires less structure in some ways and is a constant flow of delivering unfinished work to the client. There is a feeling that you are showing them a half-baked, incomplete product, and then asking the client, "What do you think so far?" and telling them, "Here's what is coming next."

As a leader of this group, the first step is to get the right people in the room. Who are the right people? Those who are involved in the process and can make or break the transition. You need the people who will buy in to the change to be there.

Start the meeting off by stating the purpose for the meeting clearly, succinctly, and in one sentence, preferably not a run-on sentence. If you can't state the purpose in one sentence, you probably don't have clarity, and if you don't have clarity and it is your meeting, they won't have clarity either.

180

THE ART OF FACILITATION

A purpose statement might sound like this:

"The purpose of this meeting is to have a discussion about the shift from Waterfall to Agile and what needs to happen so we ensure our success as a team."

It's simple, it's easy, and it is succinct.

Now here's where most leaders might turn on the projector button and start clicking on a well-prepared PowerPoint® presentation that walks their team members through the leader's thought process, the leader's ideas, and the leader's solutions, and then expects them to buy in. They may start talking *ad nauseam*, touting all of their wisdom and thoughts about the problem, the issues, their opinions, their reasoning, what they want, what they see going wrong, and what they believe the solution is to make it right. At which point they would talk for at least thirty or forty minutes and then ask if there are any questions, and since everyone is disengaged they nod, smile, and agree so they can make for the exits.

Here is another way:

Step 1: Let's say there are 12 people in the room. As the leader you tell them, I want you to get into 4 groups of 3 (yes, physically get up and move and get into a group with people you don't normally interact with as much). Next, tell them to pick a leader (person with the shortest hair, darkest eyes, etc., really doesn't matter) and then tell them that the leader is responsible for facilitating the conversation, not dominating it. Tell them their job is to make sure everyone shares and gets a chance to discuss their opinions and to be ready to discuss what they learned from the conversation with the rest of the group at the end of the exercise. It is important to stress that they don't simply regurgitate what each person said, they need to share what they learned from the conversation. Then give them the question:

"What is it about the Agile process that works well?"

CHAPTER 18

Tell them how much time they have to discuss the topic and let them go.

After the time is up, ask each leader to share what they learned and put it on the whiteboard or flip chart.

Follow up with a question to the entire group about what they see on the board or chart. Yes, let them make their own observations and come to their own conclusions.

Step 2: Tell them to change groups and get into a different group with different people. Pick a new leader and be sure to repeat the same rules and guidelines as before. It is important to not make it a complicated question. The more general the question, the greater the range of thoughts and opinions you will hear. Recall that in the Sustaining Change Model, beliefs drive behaviors and behaviors drive results. When you give the group members a broad question (just like in coaching), you are getting them to put all of their beliefs out on the table. This allows them to see the differences and/or similarities within the group. If they don't discuss these beliefs, they could get in the way and block some people from buying in or fully engaging. Just like in the Influencing Model, if you don't know where a person stands on a particular issue or topic, how do you know how to influence them?

The facilitation process is about getting the group to think as a team and work together as a team.

The next question for the group is:

"What is it about the Agile process that doesn't work well?"

Again, be sure to tell them how much time they have to discuss the topic and let them go. It is a good time to walk around and listen from a few steps away.

After the time is up, ask each leader to share what they learned and put it on the whiteboard or flip chart.

You now have two columns on the board. Ask the entire group what is it that they notice about the two lists: similarities, connections, and patterns? Invite those who may be on the quiet side to share their thoughts or opinions. And also politely discourage those who may dominate the conversation by saying, "Bob, thanks for all of your great feedback. I don't think we've heard too much from Tara...Tara?"

Again, it is important to let them make their own observations and come to their own conclusions. When they share their ideas and their thoughts, they own them, and so the buy-in will be far greater than if you were to sit in your office alone and then attempt to sell them on your wonderful idea. This is a critical point that you have to understand if you want to get your team to buy in to the solution or end result.

Step 3: Move them into larger groups, either 3 groups of 4, or 2 groups of 6. More than 6 is almost too many as I don't like to have groups larger than 5 to discuss a topic. Smaller groups are a little more intimate and it is more obvious when folks are engaging. Pick a new leader and be sure to repeat the same rules and guidelines as before. This time ask the group members to come up with either:

- The single biggest action they would need to take as a group in order to achieve the level of success they need to achieve.
- The three most impactful actions they could take as a group to achieve the results they need to achieve. (You could also have them rank order them in order of impact, urgency, or importance.)

The point is you can make it anything you want it to be, just remember that simpler is always better. Three highly important and impactful actions are easier to remember and to take away and will more than likely be more effective than ten rules or actions not done well.

After the exercise is complete, again whiteboard the responses from the teams (even the duplicates). What you do next is up to you, if you want them to rank order the responses, if you want the team to decide on the top 1, 3, or 5, or you can even ask them, "As a team, what is the next right step for us to take with the info we've gathered?"

It all comes down to what the group feels is the most impactful. If you stay a half-of-a-step back and you do not have a premeditated end in mind that you want to drive the group toward, you will get a sense of what the team thinks needs to happen to resolve the issue together.

Afterward, summarize the final list and ask if everyone is committed to putting into action what the group has created. You can ask some of the normal coaching questions to get agreement or ask what the team should do if some of the members of the team are not honoring the commitments. If this has been an issue you might ask, "How do we make sure we don't find ourselves having this same conversation two weeks from now?" or "How will this time be different?" Ask whatever question you need in order to make sure you know how to handle the situation going forward.

And lastly, make sure you ask the group, "How should we as a group check in with our progress?" Most people will probably say in the next meeting, which is just fine.

What Could Possibly Go Wrong?

As I mentioned, if you as the facilitator get stuck, you can always ask someone else in the room, "That's a great question, Bob, how would you answer it?" or "I'm not sure about that...does anyone have any ideas about that?"

The only thing that may get in your way here is you. If you can't get beyond yourself, if you feel that you need to maintain control or dominate this process, then don't waste your time or theirs. Just send an email telling them what they need to do and save yourself the meeting.

Have you ever experienced a four-hour meeting in which the leader is at the head of the table acting as if they are flying an airplane and controlling the meeting from the cockpit? Have you ever sat in a meeting where you felt you were wasting your time because you had to listen to everyone else's update (which could have been emailed) while the leader drills down into the minute details of a program that has nothing to do with you? I have...

Maybe you think I'm being harsh, yet I see it all of the time. When a leader fails to move beyond themself and their ego, you end up with ineffective meetings. Instead of being a productive collaboration, the meeting becomes a showcase for people to promote themselves. Whether they have the need to be seen as the smartest person in the room or they have to comment on the topic at hand to be seen by their higher ups, most people believe half of the meetings they attend are a waste of time.

As a leader, you have an opportunity to significantly impact other people's lives. You can utilize the people in the room to collaborate and find real solutions to the challenges facing the team, the company, or the customer. How you choose to run your meetings or facilitate a group process will determine your effectiveness as a leader. Remember that you can make a difference and help your people to grow and develop into the best version of themselves because they are experiencing their highest potential as a human being—whether you're working with them one-on-one or one-on-twenty. Facilitation is just another way of doing it powerfully and efficiently.

CHAPTER 19
THE ART OF PAINTING THE(IR) PICTURE

In 1954, well-known British artist Graham Sutherland was commissioned to paint a full-length portrait of Winston Churchill. The painting was to be a gift to Churchill from the House of Commons and the House of Lords for his 80th birthday. And, while there has been much controversy about Churchill's utter distaste of the painting, upon his first preview in which he described it as "filthy" and "malignant," Sutherland painted what he saw. When Sutherland learned that the painting for which he was paid roughly $35,000 to create was intentionally destroyed by fire in the dark of night, he condemned the destruction as an act of vandalism. The story goes that Winston was so upset about the way he was portrayed that he had the picture destroyed. Maybe it would have been a different story had he personally paid for the painting instead of receiving it as a gift. The irony here is that he believed that in destroying the painting the image would cease to exist and the poor perception others had of him in their minds would disappear along with it.

We all have an idea about how we think things should be or how they should look. They're called opinions. As a leader, we are very much enamored with our own beliefs and opinions. When it comes to influencing others, it is the opinion of others that matters much more than our own. Until we take the time to unpack and understand the opinions and beliefs of those we are trying to influence, we have no business attempting to influence them.

Understanding the gap between our beliefs and another's is a critical step in successfully getting people to buy in to an idea or solution. If you can comprehend the relationship between your opinions and another's, you can begin to understand how to approach the other party.

Sometimes in the process of influencing others, you have to help the other party see their picture, so they can make better decisions. They need to see where they may need help or where a premise or faulty belief may be preventing them from achieving their ultimate goal or desire. If you don't know what that goal or desire is, how in the world can you help them get there? I refer to this as painting their picture.

Tools to Create the Masterpiece

The image I like to imagine during the process of getting to understand how the group is perceiving things is that I am an artist. In front of me I have a blank canvas, and in my hands I have a number of brushes (tools) and the various colors of paint. When I am asking the group questions, I am then painting for them a picture of what they see, collectively as a group. The better my questions, the better I can reflect back to them what it is they believe, see, or want. These questions and their answers become data points that I am collecting so I can best understand them and they can get a visual image of the collective beliefs and opinions of their group.

The better I can help them see their ideal situation or maybe their current situation, the better they can decide what it is they need to do, shift, or change.

Your job here is to help the group or individual see a clear path out of their dilemma, a clear decision that needs to be made, or a set of actions they need to take to resolve the challenge. Remember, this isn't about you telling them what to do, it is about helping them to come to their own conclusion about the next right step.

THE ART OF PAINTING THE(IR) PICTURE

This can be tricky for some people because the natural propensity is to tell, to have the answer, to be the savior, or be the one who fixes. The odds for another person shifting or changing go up significantly if it is their choice based on their own thinking rather than your best thinking. Again, it doesn't matter so much what you think, it matters more what they think as a team of individuals who are interacting, sharing ideas, and collaborating as one.

Whether you are influencing others in a coaching session or facilitating a process, there are certain tools that you can use—brushes if you will—to create a much clearer picture for them. We can do this by focusing in on one particular area of their painting so that we can reveal a particular aspect of the painting on which the team needs to focus. The tools or techniques that follow can also be used in one-on-one coaching sessions, facilitations, and even presentations.

Compare / Contrast

Comparing and contrasting is a way to show the gap between choices or ideas. When you are attempting to influence others, you are trying to get them to move from one place to another, from one idea to another, from doing things one way to doing them a different way, or any other possibility. In order to do that, you have to highlight the gap between those two places as discussed in the Influencing Model in Chapter 17. At times it may benefit both parties if you can highlight the separation or gap that exists by comparing or contrasting the difference between the two.

By comparing and contrasting, you give the other person a framework to now see the gap in a more constructive or helpful way. This may help them to make a more informed decision on which path they need or want to take. Comparing and contrasting is all about getting clarity so that the choice or decision is more visible and allows them to make a more informed decision. The following statement is a good example:

"We can choose option A, which increases our short-term expenses but improves the long-term returns, or we can do the exact opposite

189

and decrease our expenses now, which will cost us in the future. Based on where we are currently, which is the right choice?"

At times, it is even more beneficial to magnify one side or the other of a comparison to make your point even stronger, or the gap to appear even wider. This is referred to as magnification or extrapolation.

Magnification / Extrapolation

Magnification or Extrapolation is a way to take a thought or idea and then magnify the impact or the consequences. You can do this by projecting the impact into the future, intensifying the consequences, or any other way that increases the consequences or cost of not shifting or changing.

Here is an example of what I mean: I had a client who was a leader working with a group of young engineers. One of the engineers was very disrespectful and felt that some of the things he was required to do as part of his job description were below his pay grade. The leader had been avoiding having the tough conversations over time and so the young engineer felt empowered to refuse to perform his job. As a result of one of our conversations, the leader had this conversation with his employee. Here's how he recapped the conversation to me:

Leader: "So let me see if I understand you, we agreed that these items are part of your job description and you are refusing to do them, so in essence you are saying you are not going to do your job, is that correct?"

Young Engineer: "Yes, that is correct."

Leader: "Okay great, I am going to set up a meeting with the president of the company so you can tell him of your decision. I want to make sure you have an opportunity to voice your opinion to the man who is responsible for the company. I will let you know once I get the meeting set up."

Young Engineer: "No wait, what I am saying is, I don't feel like I should have to do these tasks."

THE ART OF PAINTING THE(IR) PICTURE

Leader: "I understand exactly how you feel; I just want to give you the opportunity to voice your feelings to the president so you feel heard and you can get what you want. Do you have time tomorrow morning at 9:00? I will see if he is available."

It's difficult to believe this is an actual conversation. The point is that sometimes you have to magnify the consequences in order to help someone see how ridiculous they are being or to drive home a point. While I didn't like usurping the president's power and giving away that of the leader, he had allowed this and other issues to progress to a point based on the fact that he had failed to address them early on in the relationship.

Another form of comparing and contrasting happens when you facilitate a discussion and line up on one side of the whiteboard everything that works about a particular topic and everything that doesn't. Now the gap is apparent to everyone. You can ask questions about the cost of each one of the things that doesn't work to magnify the chasm between what does. The bigger the gap, the greater the sense of urgency or criticality, which should correlate into the importance of shifting, changing, or taking action.

4×4 Pickup

This tool is best used when you have to deliver a powerful statement that is going to sting. If you need to wake someone up, or tell them something they may not want to hear, you need to make a poignant, powerful impact that may cause bad feelings or put people in a sad, emotional place. But you can't just make them aware—or smack them on the side of the head with a 4×4 piece of wood—and then leave them there in that horrible place. You have to pick them up and move them into a place where they get relief, and that is why we refer to it as the 4×4 Pickup. Here are some examples of how to use this powerful skill in different situations:

CHAPTER 18

In a Coaching Conversation — You may get to a point where the person you are coaching just does not want to go to a place of owning responsibility for something. They may not want to accept a behavior that causes them to be seen in a bad light.

When this happens, you can simply ask them if they are open to an observation. If they say "no," which they may, you cannot proceed. However, most people will say "yes," and when they do you may respond in this way:

You: "Are you open to an observation?"

Them: "Sure."

You: "I've noticed that whenever I ask you what responsibility you have, or where you may have done something to contribute to the issues with your coworker, you either don't answer the question or you redirect and instead talk about what they did. Why is that?"

Depending on the response you can follow it up with:

You: "You know, a few years ago one of my leaders had to share an observation he had about my leadership. It was really uncomfortable, in fact I was downright pissed, and yet it was exactly what I needed to hear because I wasn't seeing it. Of course I didn't think that way at first, but after I had a chance to reflect on it, I realized it was true! It only took five years! (Or...but after a few days I realized it was true; I didn't like it, and I needed to change.)"

The idea is to make your point, and then after you have had a chance to let the information sink in, you then follow-up with a comment that diminishes the sting a bit. This follow-up comment should not be part of the initial comment, in order to allow the person to process the information and feel the uncomfortable feelings.

When you share that you have struggled with the same thing or that you didn't like getting feedback about an awareness you needed to have, you are giving them permission to own that they may have

192

THE ART OF PAINTING THE(IR) PICTURE

issues just like you did. It normalizes the situation somewhat and lets them know they are human.

When you follow up with a humorous statement that it only took you five years to own the issue, you are again humanizing the situation and being vulnerable, which should, in turn, give them permission to do the same. If you want to share that you needed to think about the feedback you received, it will give them the option to realize they might need to think about the observation you're giving them away from your meeting. The important part here is that you should never lie to your people, otherwise that is manipulation. Speak from your experience in a way that helps the other person become better. At that point, depending on where they are, you can move into what it is they need to do to resolve the issue.

In a Facilitation — Facilitation is similar to coaching. In fact, in some ways it can be a little easier because you have a few more resources to work with. After a while, you will see that being a facilitator and an observer just helps the group to see and speak about what they're experiencing as a part of the group. When everyone sees that one person is continuously hijacking the conversation and it is disrupting the process, you as the facilitator need to address this issue. Here are a couple of questions to ask the group:

> **You:** "So what are you noticing about how we're doing as a group when it comes to everyone participating?"
>
> **or**
>
> **You:** "So how are you doing as a group, in regard to everyone sharing their ideas and thoughts?"

If no one answers, wait at least a few minutes or until the silence is getting extraordinarily uncomfortable, and then after a very long pause, ask just one question:

> **You:** "Are we all sharing equally? Are we all giving others a chance to speak? If you are normally pretty vocal, are you stepping back and allowing others to share? If you normally are

CHAPTER 18

reserved in your opinions, are you stretching beyond what's comfortable and voicing your opinions or thoughts?"

If someone does make an observation, turn it into a teaching moment:

Participant: "I've noticed that some people are dominating the conversation and some haven't said a word!"

You: "Great observation, and isn't that true, that we can't always see how our behavior might be impacting the rest of the team? In one sense we may feel like we always need to comment, and in doing so we miss out on giving others a chance to speak. Can someone else share an observation?" or "What happens when everybody doesn't share?"

Participant: "We don't get to hear everyone's ideas and so we may miss out on possible solutions?"

You: "Exactly, so when you don't share, we miss out on your ideas and then you miss out on sharing your brilliance and your genius until you get back to your desk and think about all the things you wanted to share but didn't or couldn't. Of course no one hears you except yourself, and chances are you hear enough from that person!"

The idea here as a facilitator is to bring to light what everyone is experiencing in the process. You can't do this if you are so deep in the weeds or the process that you can't objectively observe. Your job is to help every person in the group to voice what they see or are experiencing, and then help them move beyond the self-imposed obstacle and toward action and agreement.

Facilitating a process or meeting can be an extremely powerful tool to achieve extraordinary results. It increases buy-in, engagement, and ownership of a group in a far greater way than you simply sharing ideas and hoping they will agree.

Recently, one of my coaching clients shared with me a story about how he facilitated a meeting. He told me that he asked three simple questions and broke up the team into groups for discussion, just like

194

THE ART OF PAINTING THE(IR) PICTURE

the process I outlined earlier in the chapter. When I asked him how it went, he told me it was amazing! When I asked him why, he said that they came up with four great ideas, and then four different members of the team volunteered to lead those actions and committed to completing them by the next meeting. I then asked how this was different from how he normally would have conducted the meeting. He told me that he would have sat in his office, come up with the ideas, shared them with the team, and then would have gone back to his office owning all four of the tasks and feeling overwhelmed to complete them by the next meeting.

The process works—if you allow it to happen. Being a leader means that the work happens in your team. When you have four people working simultaneously on four different action items, the results move from ordinary to extraordinary.

CHAPTER 20
THE ART OF WASTING TIME: MEETINGS

If I told you about an opportunity to invest in a startup company that promised an incredible return on investment, an investment that would continue expanding on a daily basis, would you want to invest?

If I told you that each and every day across the world horizon, millions of opportunities to collaborate, brainstorm, and inform or educate were right there for the taking, would you want to seize the opportunity?

Of course you would! Yet, every day these incredible opportunities to elevate the level of productivity, of learning, and solution-finding are being wasted. What is sometimes hard to believe is that most executives are aware of the problem, and yet they fail to make the changes necessary to resolve the problem. They sit down and meet to discuss the issues and yet nothing gets done. It becomes a self-perpetuating cycle, which, at times, seems like there is no end to the downward spiral.

Of course, we are talking about the dreaded m-e-e-t-i-n-g.

While some people may think that focusing on meetings is a bit basic, unproductive meetings are the number one drain on the resources of most companies. Why? Ask any executive and they will tell you that they are involved in too many meetings that are a complete

CHAPTER 20

an utter waste of time. Many times they will tell you that they show up in a meeting room and:

- Don't know the purpose of the meeting or why they are there.
- Realize after 15 minutes they didn't need to attend and could have been emailed the minutes.
- The result of this meeting is to...have another meeting.
- Realize that a number of people who need to be there aren't, and the people who are there, probably didn't have to be.
- They will be late for their next meetings, all of which are scheduled back-to-back-to-back every hour, on the hour, each in a different location.
- The time they spent in the meeting could have been cut in half if there was an agenda and folks didn't spend a lot of time hearing themselves speak.

Let me share with you a few facts and feedback that I consistently receive during our Leadership Development Program and workshops.

What a Lack of Planning Really Means

Meetings can be a great opportunity to influence others. They can also be an incredible opportunity to waste time and actually influence others in a negative way, which is in direct conflict with the intention of the one calling the meeting.

In the previous chapter, we discussed the process of facilitating a meeting and how to get folks to buy in, engage, and move toward action on a single idea.

Unfortunately, that is not what happens in most meetings that take place around the globe. Most meetings are a smorgasbord of thoughts and ideas, and many times they are unrelated to the purpose of the meeting.

Instead of being the pinnacle of collaboration and productivity, we seem to have just settled for this double-booked, over-scheduled, no agenda, too many people involved, laptops open, intermittent texting,

198

THE ART OF WASTING TIME: MEETINGS

non-decision-making meeting culture that exists in corporate America today.

I have walked into executives' offices for a meeting and met them while they were on a conference call on mute. Occasionally, we were interrupted when someone from the call asked if the executive had an opinion about the topic at hand.

Which had me wondering: how many other of the 60 or so people on the call were disengaged and multitasking their way through their emails during the call?

Studies show that approximately 11 million meetings occur in the U.S. each and every day. That said, most leaders attend about 62 or so meetings each and every month. The interesting fact here is that most folks would say that more than half of the meetings they attend are a complete waste of time. If you run the numbers, that would equate to each and every leader sitting in a room with a group of others leaders for four solid days each and every month doing nothing but wasting their time!

And yet I conduct workshop after workshop where the topic of crappy meetings and the amount of time spent in unproductive meetings is a major issue. It gets worse...

Studies show that when you are in a meeting and your cell phone is on and near you, you experience a 10-point drop in your IQ because your mind can't focus when you are thinking about, checking, and/or emailing your mother about Easter dinner. The fact is, we don't multitask well, no matter what you believe.

Coupled with studies showing the world's average IQ on the decline, we can ill afford to lower the overall level of IQ in our meetings. I don't know about you, but I can ill afford and drop in IQ; I need every 'I' and every 'Q' I can get.

So, why are we allowing our teams to spend so much time in a meeting structure that lacks focus and intention? Why would we allow this incredible brain drain and waste valuable time and not bring our best to the meeting process?

The real harm here is that in an era where most people don't have enough time to accomplish their work, we have quietly lulled ourselves into a state of faux productivity. Just because you have a roomful of people and your schedule is booked solid from 7:30 a.m. until 6:00 p.m. in meetings, doesn't mean you are accomplishing anything. In fact, the research says the exact opposite.

When you don't take the time to identify and declare the purpose of the meeting, prepare an agenda, stay on topic, or intentionally engage others in the meeting process, you are sending them the message that you do not value their time, and if you do not value their time, you do not value them! How else would they interpret a message in which your actions communicate that they are not valued?

Stating a problem without a solution really doesn't change anything. What is needed is a system or set of guidelines to address this issue so that you can start leveraging your time, energy, resources, and team.

The 5 Immutable Laws of Conducting Meetings

Rule #1: Define the Meeting Purpose Before You Schedule a Meeting
Before you even think about sending out a meeting invite, ask yourself these five questions:
1. Why am I having this meeting?
2. Am I clear about the key points/topics for the agenda?
3. Do I have to have a meeting to accomplish my objective? Is there another format that could work? Email, memo, short conversation, etc.
4. Who needs to be there, and can they attend?
5. Who doesn't need to be there? Really?

Rule #2: Always, Always, Always Have an Agenda
Every meeting should have an agenda. It can be a 1-page outline shared in advance (minimally two days in advance) or an email in bulleted point format explaining the following:

- Purpose for the meeting (in one sentence)
- Time requirements overall
- Specific times to discuss specific topics and who owns that topic for this meeting
- Preparation needed and what you are requiring the participants to do in advance and during the meeting (decide, buy-in, start, stop, etc.)

Rule #3: Agree on Rules for Engagement
- Decide as a group how you will handle accountability (or lack of).
- Decide as a group how you will make decisions.
- Decide as a group what happens if the meeting guidelines are not being honored.

Here are a few ideas that some groups I have worked with implemented to overcome some of the challenges they were experiencing:

1. If you don't receive an agenda at least one day prior to the meeting you do not attend the meeting (all agendas required, the Rule #2 checklist).
2. No cell phones on or present.
3. Meetings don't end on the hour and are not automatically an hour in length.
4. If you are late you pay $20 and state the reason you were late as: "The reason I was late is that my time is more valuable than yours." (Yes, you kept people waiting because you chose to be somewhere else, fine, just pay the fine and sit down).
5. No laptops—even for taking notes. Notes come from the designated note taker.
6. You cannot overbook a meeting on someone else's schedule.
7. You must send out any pre-meeting reading materials at least two days before the meeting.
8. Only those who have an active role in the meeting need to be present, otherwise they are sent the meeting minutes, if it was

deemed necessary to keep them in the loop of communication. It is *their* responsibility to read the meeting notes.

9. If someone takes the meeting off-agenda, anyone in the meeting can speak to that point and redirect the group back to the agenda topic or time if the leader isn't doing so. This can be done in the form of a question, "Can you help me understand how that point or topic is relevant to the specific agenda item we are currently discussing?"

Rule #4: Honor the Meeting Schedule

- Choose someone to take meeting minutes to capture the important information, decisions, or actions items.
- Stay on schedule, even if it means starting before everyone is there.
- Don't leave a topic without an action item and who owns it.
- Recap the decisions, action items, and next steps.
- End on time.

Rule #5: Follow-Up After the Meeting

- Provide the meeting info to the attendees and anyone else who needs the info. Be brief, here's what happened, will happen, by whom, and by when.

Sometimes when things seem to be out of control, for example everyone's calendar is booked and double booked with meetings, you have to go back to the basics and come up with a simple solution. In order to do that, you have to make things black and white, which will require some difficult decisions. As complicated as we can make the topic of meetings, the fact is everyone struggles with the topic and very few people are willing to make the hard calls.

If you don't do anything, you and your team will continue to discuss and complain about all the meetings they have to attend and the quality of those meetings. The fact is that ineffective meetings are more of a leadership issue than a time management issue. It is more

THE ART OF WASTING TIME: MEETINGS

of an issue about how we value ourselves and each other than it is a logistics issue. And, while this process seems so incredibly simple, we complicate the problem by continuing to believe that it is unsolvable. It is solvable if you as the leader are willing to take the lead and make the hard call to change the meeting culture on your team or in your organization.

The worst thing that could happen by utilizing this simple process is that it would eliminate a lot of useless meetings. Why? Because people would think through the process of having, planning, and deciding whether they even needed to have a meeting.

The best thing that could happen by utilizing this process is that you create a meeting culture that is rooted in valuing your team members and their time, and about achieving results. Those two things are inseparable, you can't have one without the other.

CHAPTER 21

THE ART OF PRESENTING

The Art of Presenting is to help others see your picture in a way that allows them to connect to you or your story, in a way that they can feel or experience.

You are determining what you want them to see on the canvas, and yet, you have to take into consideration that they may have a different picture or vision in mind. You invite them to lean in and see what you see, to walk them down a path so they can see things in a new way or hear new information, in a way that will benefit, teach, or inspire them.

Painting Your Picture: Influencing 1 on 100+

First, let's state a known fact: This format of influencing is by far the most stressful for people. The idea of standing in front of 100 people with all eyes on you can be extremely daunting. While some people bask in the limelight, others may shrink at the idea of speaking in public. Fear of speaking actually has a scientific name; it is called "glossophobia." Glossophobia is the fear of public speaking. The word glossophobia comes from the Greek *glōssa*, meaning tongue, and *phobos*, fear or dread.

That said, if you have to speak, you may as well do it as best as you can. If you follow a few simple formulas and ideas presented here, you can significantly increase your ability to influence others in this venue. You just need to be aware of some of the pitfalls and have a few basic skills tucked under your belt.

Miss-takes: How Do Things Go Wrong?

One of the biggest mistakes people make when preparing for a presentation is that they feel the need to present more information than is needed to ensure their point gets across to the audience.

The information or the PowerPoint® presentation becomes a wall or shield that they can hide behind because the idea of getting up in front of an audience without them is scary. So, they try to cover more than they can and in doing so, they may confuse their audience by overloading them with too many points or too many slides.

When this happens, it becomes more about the presenter feeling comfortable than it does about the audience getting a great message or receiving value. This is what we referred to in the Power vs. Force Model of Leadership when we are self-centered versus other-centered. The point of a presentation is not about making sure you feel shielded behind an arsenal of data, it is about giving the audience an experience.

Another mistake people make is the notion that they have to be funny to gain the attention of others and so they begin with a joke that they recently heard. They tell the joke, they get a chuckle, and then check off the "need to be funny" box on their presentation checklist. Many times the joke has no connection to the material, and if it did, the presenter doesn't make the connection to the audience so that it is relevant; it was just a joke duct-taped to the presentation to check off a box.

Sometimes a presenter will apologize for the fact that they don't present often or this isn't something they like to do, or apologize in advance if the presentation isn't good. When you do this, you are pre-

206

THE ART OF PRESENTING

senting from a place of weakness. You are again focusing on what's going on within you rather than what needs to happen within your audience.

Understand the idea behind it: "If I play small I will gain some sympathy in advance if I screw up." That's about emotional safety. However, all the presenter is really doing is diluting their message.

What you most need to remember here is that you need to give your audience a compelling reason to listen. The most compelling reason you can give them is that you have something they need to hear— something that will make their life better, less painful, less stressful, less problematic, or help them make more money, become quicker, faster, or better. You simply have to start by grabbing their attention and engage them enough to have them say: "Okay I'll give you a chance, or I will listen, because I think what you have to say will help me!

Getting Buy-In

Getting buy-in needs to happen in the first minute or so of your presentation, so it behooves you to not spend an enormous amount of time on jokes, apologies, or anything else that takes away from giving the audience a reason to listen.

I find that skipping over the niceties and jumping right into the story or the facts is a powerful way to command attention and get the audience to start buying in—that is, as long as the information is compelling.

The most important factor to consider when getting an audience to buy in is to know and understand what the audience already believes about your topic. What are their preconceived notions and opinions about what you're going to tell them?

For example, if you are presenting a new program for centralizing a process into one department (your department) and the audience is highly vested in a decentralized model because they want to maintain control, keep head count, or it's just plain politics, then you need to seriously think about that before you begin. You need to know your audience well enough to know what you're up against!

This may mean you have to be more realistic with regard to what you are asking them to do. It means you have to create an experience that compares and contrasts the high risk of leaving it completely decentralized, and one that quells their fears of moving to a completely centralized system that causes them to experience their greatest fear (loss of head count, loss of control, etc.).

Instead of trying to get them to commit to working with a centralized system, your best chance to get buy-in is to create a balance of centralized and decentralized, a halfway point or a meeting halfway solution. A middle of the road solution that gets them to move away from the old way of doing things to a new way that allows them to maintain a sense of control without surrendering it all. If you don't know your audience and what's realistic for them to buy in to, or if you don't know their pain points (fears), it's going to be a really painful presentation for you and for them.

Getting buy-in during a presentation is no different than getting buy-in in a coaching situation or a facilitation format. You have to create an emotional connection to the subject matter. People buy more on emotion then they do logic. And while logic or data does play a part, in the end, it is how someone feels about the buying decision, about how their life will be better, more productive, less stressful, etc. Utilizing emotion is a critical piece in getting others to move toward you or your ideas.

As we learned earlier, when you ask people questions, you engage their brain and get them thinking. If they're thinking, they will more than likely feel some emotion tied to those thoughts, and once you do that, your job is to leverage those emotions or feelings in order to get them to move toward you and your ideas.

For example, if I utilize the earlier example regarding the centralization of a process, I can start by telling a story about an incident that happened at another company (regardless of the industry) where there was significant brand damage or financial hardship on the company.

THE ART OF PRESENTING

I would seek the biggest, most expensive situation I could find. If I was talking about a process to centralize a system to identify security breaches or systems going down, I would use an example of a multi-million-dollar loss to ABC company and the financial impact on the brand reputation. It doesn't matter if it was in the same industry, I would make a connection to our organization by using a what-if question:

"What if this incident took place here at our company? What would the impact be to our bottom line? How would you feel if that was our name all over the nightly news or on the front page of the Wall Street Journal?"

This makes an emotional connection with the audience and nudges them slightly toward the possibility that it could happen and that we have an opportunity to prevent it.

Now the audience is more likely to listen to what you have to say. You have created an emotional experience and got them to buy in enough to listen...for a while.

You also need to realize, that at this point, some people in the audience (especially the naysayers, i.e. the folks who are highly invested in keeping things exactly the way they are) will be sitting there and mentally listing all the reasons why it wouldn't happen in their department or at their organization. These are the obstacles that will prevent you from influencing them and prevent them from having to change.

This is the perfect time to acknowledge those very obstacles and place some doubt in their minds. It is also a time to let them know that you are not oblivious to what they're thinking, that you have thought through this process, and that you've done your homework.

For example, you could say something like this:

"Now I am sure that a number of you are saying to yourselves that a breach or breakdown that occurred at ABC company could never happen here at our company. I can't help but think that there were a few folks at ABC company here that said the same things to themselves."

Or

"Now I am wondering how many of you are sitting there and thinking, we've never had an issue, and besides the current system is working fine (pause)...I'm sure the leaders at ABC company felt the same way (slight pause) until they picked up the Wall Street Journal that morning. You never think it's going to happen to you...until it does...and then it's too late. What I want to talk to you about today is..."

This is why it is critical that you do your research before you present. As we discussed in the Influencing Model, you must know where the audience stands in relationship to where you want or need them to go if you are going to be successful in influencing them at all.

The Power of Story: The Me—You Connection

One of the most powerful and compelling skills you can use when presenting and influencing is to tell a story. The story needs to be able to stir some type of emotion in the audience or allow them to relate to the story in some way. Whatever the emotion is, you need to be able to get the audience to make an emotional connection.

I like to think that if I am going to share a story, I am not sharing a story about me, I am sharing a story about them. This is why sharing a personal story about yourself or your family can help them connect.

Why? They have families, they have spouses, and partners and kids, and parents, so they can connect to their families through stories about yours. This is one reason why comedians are funny. When they tell real-life stories about their crazy relative or friend, everyone has a crazy person in their family or their life, so the audience can relate. The story of your crazy Uncle John is the story of their crazy Uncle Bob.

Your story could be as short as two minutes or as long as seven to ten minutes. Whether it be happy and humorous or sad, the audience members need to find some connection to your words.

THE ART OF PRESENTING

One of the great things about being brought up in an Italian Catholic family is that it makes for great stories. The stereotypical dominating, over-controlling, beat-you-within-an-inch-of-your-life, Italian mother resonates with most people. And, when the truth is that your mother was actually 5'10", played volleyball and her nickname was "Spike," it makes sense that occasionally we were the ball...it simply works! And no one else can tell that story. There is a joke in the speaking business about the Starfish story. It's a story that has been told so many times that audiences groan when they hear it. No one can tell the story about my mother, except my brother—and he's an accountant.

Going back and thinking about stories that you faced as a parent, or as a child, that are relatable to most people will help you make a connection to the audience. It makes you relatable and inches them closer to you and your ideas or whatever message you're trying to communicate. That is as long they can make the connection.

The underlying idea here is that you share a story that only you can tell, and yet everyone relates to it because it is real, genuine, believable, and relevant to your topic or point.

Here's a formula for making your stories relevant.

S.P.A.: A Foolproof Story Formula

Years ago, I worked with a woman who impacted my life incredibly. Her name is Glenna Salsbury and she is a fellow speaker and coach. I hired her to coach me and she ended up becoming an extraordinary friend and mentor. She shared with me a formula for telling stories and it forever changed the way I speak.

The concept of S.P.A. stands for Story, Point, and Application. Meaning, tell your story, make your point, and then close the gap between your story and how it applies to the audience. It doesn't matter if your story is two minutes long or twenty.

I was working with a group of salespeople who sold cat litter. This was a newer product line for them and they were looking to expand

CHAPTER 21

their market share into some of the larger retailers like Target and Costco.

They hadn't been all that well known in the retail market, but for years had been a big player in selling clay-based products to some of the largest and most famous baseball stadiums in the United States. They had also been in business for well over seventy-five years.

As you know, when you get an appointment with a buyer from Target, you have a very small window of time to impress them.

I asked one of the sales reps to show me how they built credibility with buyers and shared the history of the company. I asked how he told the story of the company in order to show longevity and that they'd been around for a while.

He proudly proceeded to pull out a tripod flip chart, like the one an air conditioner salesperson puts on your kitchen table when all you really want is the specs and the price. He starts telling me about what happened seventy-five years ago and how so and so's grandfather started out as a small company selling sawdust to machine shops to absorb moisture and spills (flip) and then he (flip) after he (flip)...ten minutes later I was like...borrrrrr...inggggggg...you lost me at hello!

Here's what I asked the salesperson: Could you accomplish the same point by sharing this story with the buyer?

> *"Seventy-five years ago when our President's grandfather starting selling sawdust to machine shops to absorb oil, I'm sure he never thought our products would be in every major baseball stadium in the country, and I'm sure he never thought we'd be revolutionizing the cat litter industry at a major U.S. retailer like Target!"*

I told a story, I made my point and I made relevant why I was in the buyer's office all in less than a minute.

You see it doesn't have to be lengthy, it could be very short, sweet, and to the point and yet extremely powerful.

You can alter the story interchangeably with the point, meaning you can make your point and then share a story that demonstrates the

THE ART OF PRESENTING

point followed up by the application. You have to remember, that you need to close that gap and help them make the jump as to how it applies to them.

Recall the earlier example and the process: you tell a story, you make the point, and then the question you ask, "What if that happened here?" is the connector that makes it applicable to your audience.

What you will find is that some of your stories can be used in a number of different situations depending on the point you're trying to make. The point and application will vary based on how you connect the story and the point to their work and their life. This is how it could sound if you wanted to talk about stress and balancing family life.

For example:

"Have you ever had one of those days where it seemed like everything that could go wrong—did? I was having a miserable day. Everything was falling apart; it was one thing after another. It was such a busy day at the office and I was so busy, I had to skip lunch, so I walked in the house starving and wondering what was for dinner (pause).

I walk in the door whereupon my wife thrusts, sorry...throws my 3-year-old son into my arms. He is covered with illegible writing all over his face and arms. In his left hand is a giant sharpie marker and she says while thrusting him at me, (pause) "If you don't kill him, I will," and then she walks away. It was at that exact moment in time that I realized that if I wanted to live, my best option was to call a babysitter and take my wife out to dinner (pause). McDonald's...Burger King...a French Bistro...didn't matter...she needed out and she needed out now!

I could make the following applications:

1. How many of you struggle at times with the ability to *not* take the stress from the office home with you and allow it to negatively impact your spouse, your partner, or your kids? Show of hands. Today, I want to talk to you about how to do a better job of leaving work at work...

2. How many times do you and your team lay out a plan and think this is the best plan ever...as long as we follow it and

213

don't change it? And then something happens, the situation changes unexpectedly, and you have to do a 180-degree-turnaround to the plan? Today, I want to talk to you about our ability to adjust as a team with the continuous shifts we've been experiencing in our project's priorities...

3. Your ability to read the emotional context of what is happening in a room at any given moment will determine your ability to overcome some of the challenges you're currently facing! Today I want to talk about...

As you can see, those are three different applications or pivot points from the same story. As long as you make it applicable to the people you're speaking to, it will work. And, chances are, they have experienced something similar in their own story at some time.

Tools to Enhance Your Masterpiece

These tools were mentioned in the facilitation chapter. You can use some of these same tools in your presentations to increase your level of influence and the audience's level of buy-in.

Compare & Contrast

Comparing and contrasting in a presentation helps to clarify your audience's perspective. It allows you to provide options for them to think through, so they can decide what makes more sense or which idea they should buy in to.

When I am utilizing the compare and contrast technique, I find it most impactful if I make the point and then move to the diametrically opposed view, for example. This creates the widest gap possible and separates the two points as far as I need to in order to help them make their decision to buy in or not. The wider the gap, the more distinctive and separate the ideas are. When I offer a solution, I am closing that gap by showing them how my solution eases the stress, pain, churn, or loss.

THE ART OF PRESENTING

For example, if I am talking about our earlier example with the centralization or decentralization of the IT Process and I know this is a prickly issue, here's how I would present it:

"On one hand, we could go to a 100% decentralized system which allows each of the separate departments to be 100% responsible for their own system and provides full departmental autonomy. This is the system that was utilized at ABC Company which resulted in the system breakdown because the silos didn't allow the various departments to talk to each other."

"On the other hand, we could go to a 100% centralized system which ensures that all the interrelated pieces and parts would be connected because they would all be in the same department. This would ensure that we could avoid the same meltdown that ABC Company experienced. However, you would more than likely lose head count, relinquish total control, and I would be run out of town tied to the back of a car!"

(Yes, that last sentence contained a 4×4 Pickup component to relieve the audience's fear by inserting humor. Starting to get the picture?).

This creates a situation in which the audience is aligning somewhere along the spectrum between one end and the other with some semblance of an emotional connection. Once I present the contrast, I can then offer the option I am interested in because it is a step in the right direction. Remember, I know they will never go for a 100% option either way. Next, I would propose Option C in a question format.

"But what if there was another possibility? What if there was a way to get the best of both worlds? A way that allows you to continue to influence the process but ensure that all the departments were connected and communicating to each other so we reduced the possibility of a meltdown like the one at ABC Company by 80%?"

Then, I would present my idea while making sure I continued to compare this choice to both of the previous choices to enhance the third option. Now for some of you this would probably seem like a no-brainer. That said, most leaders, especially those leaders who are more task-oriented or data driven, would not take the time to lay out the options, they would simply present their plan without taking the time to compare, contrast, and influence this way because they believe the data speaks for itself, or the process speaks for itself, but it doesn't! You have to stir some emotion, if you want to influence others.

This is an art, you don't slap paint on a canvas and say *voila*, it's a masterpiece! So don't slap words on a PowerPoint® deck and expect to get buy-in and expect for people to jump in line behind you to sign up.

Extrapolation / Magnifying

Extrapolation and magnification are very useful tools in a presentation as well. For example, if we stay with the example regarding the centralization discussion and you wanted to magnify the impact of a system malfunction or breach, you could say something like:

> *"The system was down at ABC Company for two days until the engineers and IT folks could locate the cause of the problem. This resulted in a 3-million-dollar revenue loss because customers were unable to place orders online, and so they were forced to call in and place orders over the phone with a customer service agent.*
>
> *Now let's think about this for a second, put yourself in the shoes of the customer. Imagine if all of our customers had to start calling in their orders starting right this second? How many people would simply hang up and go to the competition?*
>
> *How many people would continue to do business after they found out that their credit card info had been breached at our company? Do you think giving them a year of LifeLock® is going to repair the damage to our brand? How do you even put a price on that?"*

Taking the time to make sure you emphasize the pain points that are also the cost points allows you to tip the scale in favor of your solution.

Simply providing the data without magnifying its negative effect doesn't increase your ability to influence as much as you may need to, in order to get them to shift.

Remember people don't like change, especially change in which some type of loss is perceived, whether it be control, head count, job security, influence, or a blow to their ego. Let's face it, as leaders, sometimes it is our egos that get in our way.

4×4: Pickup

Some people find that if they want to make a presentation more memorable or a point more impactful, they need to tell story that is dramatic or inspirational. The idea is that the audience will be stirred to feel happy, sad, inspired, motivated, or whatever emotion the speaker is attempting to stir.

I think we have all seen, at one time or another, a presentation that was meant to inspire and move us to action. In fact, if you watch television and see the ads for world hunger or American Society for the Prevention of Cruelty to Animals (ASPCA), their sole purpose is to stir your emotions. The idea is that you will be inspired to take action and to feel good about it because you helped those poor animals by making a contribution. The relief is that you feel better when you take action and you help others.

As a professional speaker, I have been in a number of programs in which the presenter is telling a sad story to the point of getting emotional on stage with the idea of also stirring up emotion in the audience. I have talked to speakers who judge the success of their presentation on whether or not people in the audience tear up or get emotional.

For the record, I think this is presenter malpractice. In the speaking profession, if you can't tell a story without getting overly emotional, it's probably best not to tell the story.

If you do, however, tell an emotionally sad story to make a point, you have to follow it up afterward with a dose of humor or some way to bring the audience back to a neutral state. Telling a story that

CHAPTER 21

leaves the audience in a low spot is just plain wrong. It goes back to the Power vs. Force Model as it pertains to being other-centered versus being self-centered, so unless it is a eulogy at a funeral, I highly recommend you don't practice this.

It can be good, however, to interject humor in your presentation.

Humor

Utilizing humor is a great way to engage the audience in your presentation. It can liven up what would otherwise be a very flat presentation and make it more enjoyable for your audience. It has to be more than just telling a joke and checking off the box that says, "be funny." It needs to be authentic.

Telling a story that utilizes self-deprecating humor is safe. I have seen instances in which a speaker used sarcasm at the expense of someone in the audience or a group of people that ended up backfiring on them and put a huge gap between the presenter and their audience. This is similar to the way that off-color humor or profanity can put off some audiences. It is always best to default to the safer side when it comes to those decisions.

I find that the best stories I have told are those that people can relate to and are real events that have actually happened to me. If you look back at the stories you tell around the family table that make everyone laugh, it works. If you look at stories about growing up and being awkward or feeling left out as a teenager, it works. Why? Because everyone had those same experiences. If they say they didn't, they're lying. Your kids do funny things, say funny things, so use those stories. Why? Because anyone with kids has moments just like yours. Just be sure to relate it to a point and help them understand how it is applicable to them, their work, or their challenges.

Call-Backs

Utilizing a call-back during your presentation is a skill you that can bring an audience to relate back to a previous point or to pick them up after a 4×4.

THE ART OF PRESENTING

If you tell a humorous story early on, you can refer back to the punch line or a certain aspect of the story that they would remember. This is referred to as a callback and can be very impactful, especially if you are following up after an intense point.

I tell a story in the very beginning of one of my presentations about going to a jewelry store for a surprise engagement ring and being shown a ring that had a $25,000 price tag on it. After sheepishly asking for something a bit less expensive—like about $23,000 less expensive—I hand the ring back to the salesperson.

Later I utilized the fact that I bought a smaller ring into a story about 9/11 a bit later in the program to make sure the audience is not left down in the sadness of 9/11. By referring to the fact that my wife at the time was squeezing my hand so intensely, I was glad I bought the smaller ring, because the big rock might have cost me a finger. They remember the story and they laugh again, and, more importantly, they aren't left wallowing in the sadness of a tragic event.

The Pause

One of the most powerful tools you can use during any interaction with another person is the pause. You may have noticed that during some of my writing I will use an ellipsis to put a pause in a sentence. I find my words flow better that way than to simply write the word (pause) or (long pause). This refers to pace. There is a well-known speech coach in the world of professional speakers by the name of Lou Heckler. Lou has dedicated a great deal of time coaching speakers to leverage the power of the pause.

I was once working with a leader who is incredibly smart, very knowledgeable, and very personable. Bob is an IT Architect, and as far as architects go, Bob is one of the most personable technical people I know, and has a high IQ and a high EQ as well.

We were discussing influence and impact, and while he was speaking, I realized how much more impactful and influential his message would be if...he...just...slowed...down...and paused between his words.

When you make a point, tell a funny story, then make another point, let it sit and simmer. Let the audience laugh before you start up again or make ...the...next...point!

Yes, this sounds simple, yes it is easy, and yes it is extremely powerful.

Book-Ending

Book-ending is a way to reiterate a point that you make in the beginning of your presentation and then follow it up or revisit it at the end of the presentation. The idea is to bring closure or bring the audience back to the main point with which you began.

One way of doing this is to open with a story and not complete the story. Just be sure to end at a point where you can make a logical transition to the application that was discussed in the S.P.A. process earlier in the chapter.

Book-ending, when done properly, can give the audience a sense of completion. It can be a logical closing that aligns the points you made throughout your presentation to move your audience into action.

One way of doing this is to ask the question or make the point that gets the audience thinking back about your initial story.

Here's one way of doing it in the context of the ABC Company:

"Now some of you might be wondering...so how did ABC Company respond to the meltdown? How did they get back on track? Well here's what happened..."

Yes, it is best if the story aligns with your desired option. If it doesn't, you can make the case that they never recovered and since then they have had to work extremely hard to overcome the damage that was done to the company and the brand.

This technique reminds them of the possible change that could happen if they do not change the system, or the happy ending if they do. It also brings your presentation full circle, back to where you started, except now they are hopefully seeing things with a brand new perspective.

As I referenced earlier, it was T.S. Eliot who said: "We shall not cease from exploration, and the end of all our exploring will be to arrive where we started and know the place for the first time."

Hopefully, you have taken them on a journey with your presentation so that at the end of it, they have more information, so they can make better decisions, and it is because you influenced them to see things differently. You painted a different picture for them to see the same issue they've struggled with for a while, and now they see it in a completely different way.

Finishing Touches

The most important thing to remember is that you need to be very intentional about why you are presenting, what you are presenting, and to whom you are presenting. Getting up and winging it doesn't really work, regardless of what you believe about how good you are as a presenter.

You have to remember that the opportunity to stand up in front of a group and have their attention is like leadership in the way that the audience does not have to listen or buy in just because you are standing up there and talking.

It is a privilege to lead and it is a privilege to have the opportunity to present. How well you choose to prepare determines how much you value your audience's time, and that is a direct reflection of how much you value your audience.

If you don't value them or their time you certainly can't expect them to turn around and value your opinions or your insights.

Utilizing presentations to influence others can be extremely powerful—if it is done right. Utilizing these skills will increase your ability to influence a greater number of folks than just facilitating a small group or a one-on-one coaching session.

You just have to be willing to walk through the steps and be intentional about becoming a leader who influences when presenting.

CHAPTER 21

Practicing the Art
Creating the Stories

Think back to significant events that have changed the way you look at work, life, or business.

Utilizing the S.P.A. process, craft a story that you could tell in less than three minutes.

Create three different points to the story along with three different applications. Remember the application is just closing the gap and making the point and the story relevant to the audience.

Bonus: Think of an event that happened at work in the past week that would be a good story to share, and that would make a point you could use in an upcoming meeting. Make sure it is less than three minutes in total to tell the story, make the point, and communicate how it relates to the audience or group.

SUMMARY

A Tale of Two Leaders

Once upon a time there was a leader who was driven by success. She was an incredible producer and she was promoted to a leadership role because she got results. She was driven by success and success was defined by her title, her income, and the size of her office. She went out of her way to tell folks about her accomplishments. She always felt the need to pontificate in meetings or presentations about her vast knowledge and experience while she shot down the ideas of others. In large meetings, about two-thirds of the way through, she would stand up and pontificate about all she knew and why the presenter was wrong. As soon as she opened her mouth, people pulled out their cell phones, laptops, and mentally checked out. And although people smiled and patted her on the back, behind the scenes she was despised. She stayed stuck in her position for years because her leaders tolerated her and her peers evaluated her poorly. Her ego and self-centeredness leaked into every facet of her personal life as well, and soon her husband left her. Her children never thought much of her as a mother because she always placed her needs and her career above the needs of her family. Over time they eventually pushed her out of their lives.

She died, alone, in a nursing home. Her ego and self-centeredness had driven everyone away from her, including her best self. In the end, you could say that she squandered a life of significance and instead drove herself toward a life of so-called success.

Once upon a time there was a great leader whose purpose and focus was to bring out the best in all of his people. He focused on asking great questions and helping them discover how they were getting in their own way. He asked those questions that made them think and at times he even made them uncomfortable. He called them to play bigger when they were fearful and wanted to shrink down. He chose to believe in them even in the times when they doubted themselves. He prided himself on the fact that folks came into his department, (eventually his division) and were promoted, some leaving the company and going into other organizations and duplicating their success.

He became known as a developer of people and he taught his leaders how to develop more leaders. He was tough at times because he wanted people to break out of their comfort zones and become the best version of themselves possible. Collectively, the impact and results achieved by the teams and leaders he developed were no less than extraordinary.

One day, close to the end of his life, he was lying in bed in a nursing home, surrounded by his family. There was a soft knock on the door and in walked a middle-aged man in a great looking suit. The leader opened his eyes, vaguely remembering the face, although he remembered it being much younger.

The man walked to the side of the bed and said, "(Your name), I don't know if you remember me, it has been quite a few years but I used to work for you at XYZ Company. I had heard you were sick and I realized that I never ever thanked you for what you taught me when I was a young leader. I remember how at first you would ask me questions I didn't think I knew the answers to, but you made me think about what I wanted and the importance of making it about my people and less about me. There was one time when I was going to throw in the towel because I didn't believe I could really lead a team, and you asked me a question I have never forgotten." You said, "If I was getting the results with my people that I wanted, would I still want to be a leader?" I didn't have to even think about it, I knew the answer in a nanosecond. That moment changed my life because I knew I was called to lead others; I just didn't know how, until I worked for you. Thank you for believing in me when I couldn't believe in myself. You made a huge difference in my life and the lives of those I lead." He gave him a soft hug and left.

You can chase success or you can pursue significance. Being a leader means that you get the privilege of making a significant impact on the lives of those you interact with—whether you lead them at the office, at the nonprofit board you serve on, or your kids' baseball team. You just have to get out of your own way...

Every day you write the script for how your story ends.
Which script are you writing?

Your Leadership Story

Recall the story about Michelangelo and the creation of the *David*. When he created his sculptures, Michelangelo always envisioned the art that was buried underneath the rock and stone. In his mind, he just needed to remove the rock to reveal the brilliance that lay dormant underneath it.

Like Michelangelo removing the rock to reveal the brilliance that lies dormant below the surface, your role as a leader is to influence others to draw out their brilliance and uncover, or, quite possibly, rediscover *their* hidden brilliance.

Sometimes, that brilliance or genius has been covered up by years of old beliefs that no longer serve the person, however they still cling to them out of a false sense of security or comfort they get by playing small, shrinking down, or hiding.

Influencing others means that you help them to see the obstacles

EXTRAORDINARY RESULTS

that they are placing on their paths and then help them to remove those obstacles if that is what they choose to do. You cannot do it for them.

Sometimes removing the obstacles happens quickly and similar to the way Michelangelo removed the rock to reveal the hidden brilliance. Sometimes it seems painstakingly slow or tedious in the same way the restorers removed the dirt and the grime that was masking the true beauty of the stone little by little.

Between May of 2001 and July 2015, Wells Fargo salespeople created more than 2 million fake bank accounts or credit cards that were opened without their customers' knowledge. On September 8, 2016, the Consumer Financial Protection Buruea (CFPB), the Los Angeles City Attorney, and the Office of the Comptroller (OCC) fined the bank $185 million dollars.

Over time, these fake transactions generated millions and millions of dollars in fees from customers, while simultaneously generating millions of dollars in bonuses for the leaders at the top of the heap.

When they got caught, these leaders turned on their own team members, blamed their employees, and 5,300 of them. On September 22, 2016, two employees filed a lawsuit in a California Superior Court, alleging that employees were "either demoted, forced to resign, or terminated" for not meeting the "impossible" quotas the bank set as goals for employees to open accounts on behalf of customers. The irony of this situation is that it occurred not too long after the housing bubble bust, in which Wells Fargo also played a part along with a few other big banks.

Of course, while this story was unfolding we experienced grandstanding upon grandstanding by every senator and congressman about the outrage of this fraud.

A year after this story was first reported in September of 2016, and over the course of the year, behind all of the positioning and public announcements of changes in customer policies and promises to do better, a morning headline began with: "Wells Fargo is back in the spotlight for another scandal. This time, for signing up 490,000 auto-loan customers for insurance they didn't need."

And, the original number first reported in September of 2016 was recently adjusted to reflect a more accurate number. The actual number of "potentially unauthorized" customer accounts that were opened was actually 3.7 million. A 67% increase over the original 2.1 million figure.

Being a leader and making the right choices and doing the right thing for your team and your customers is not always easy in this landscape.

Surviving in a corporate world that is sometimes filled with politics and mistrust, and doesn't always reward the long-term development of people can be difficult; and staying the course may feel like an impossibility at times. It is much easier to focus on the short-term gains and profits, at the expense of the people.

Like great art, great leaders withstand the test of time. They weather the storms of life and the never-ceasing wave of change. They continue to persevere and to perfect their skills, even after they have been moved up front to the center of the Plaza.

Great leaders know they need to take the time to get off the world's stage and restore themselves carefully in a way that heals instead of damages. And lastly, extraordinary leaders need the vision to see beyond *what it is* to the brilliance of *what it could be* in themselves and in each individual they lead.

The story of David and Goliath dates back to the year 1028 B.C. If records are right, that would make David about twelve years old at that time when historians estimate his encounter with Goliath took place.

Two thousand, five-hundred and thirty-two years later, Michelangelo would sculpt the world-famous statue of *David* that sits in the Academia in Florence, Italy, and is seen by millions of people every year and has for a very long time. Each of them has their own story, their place in his-story and yet they are connected in an unusual way—a way that continues to impact others all these years later.

You have your own story, and each one of your team members has their own story. Each and every day, you have an opportunity to connect these stories in a way that can be extremely powerful.

Each and every day you can influence others, whether 1-on-1,

EXTRAORDINARY RESULTS

1-on-10, or 1-on-100. You now know that you cannot force people to change, to be different, or to be motivated—but you can influence them. And who knows what you might inspire them to be or to do? Then, imagine that they inspire others in the same way you influenced them and on and on and...

Imagine the extraordinary results that could be achieved!

Remember that leaders are pathfinders. Remember that you can't inspire others to get on their path if you are lost and have fallen off yours.

David, throughout his life, was on and off the path. In the end, he died while on his path, and in doing so he inspired an artist to tell his story thousands of years later in a statue. And it was that artist's work who inspired me and countless others to follow the leadership path.

It is my deepest hope that something you have read in this book, some idea that was shared with you, will inspire you and then allow you to do the same with those you lead.

REFERENCES

Arnold, C. (2017, August 02). Who snatched my car? Wells Fargo did. Retrieved August 10, 2017, from http://www.npr.org/2017/08/02/541182948/who-snatched-my-car-wells-fargo-did

Asplund, J., M.A., Lopez, S. J., Ph.D., Hodges, T., Ph.D., & Harter, J., Ph.D. (2005,2007). The research behind StrengthsFinder 2.0. Retrieved August, 2017, from http://strengths.gallup.com/private/Resources/CSFTechnicalReport031005.pdf

Blake, P. (n.d.). Timeline of the Wells Fargo accounts scandal. Retrieved August 10, 2017, from http://abcnews.go.com/Business/timeline-wells-fargo-accounts-scandal/story?id=42231128

Bocchio, M., McHugh, S. B., Bannerman, D. M., Sharp, T., & Capogna, M. (2016, April 05). Serotonin, amygdala and fear: Assembling the puzzle. Retrieved August 08, 2017, from https://www.ncbi.nlm.nih.gov/pubmed/27092057

Botelho, E.L., Powell, K.R., Kincaid, S., and Dina Wang. (2017, July 18). Four things that set successful CEOs apart. Retrieved August 02, 2017, from https://hbr.org/2017/05/what-sets-successful-ceos-apart

Branden, N. (2004). *The six pillars of self-esteem*. New York: Bantam.

Bregman, P. (2014, July 23). How (and why) to stop multitasking. Retrieved August 10, 2017, from https://hbr.org/2010/05/how-and-why-to-stop-multitaski.html

Contrera, J. (2014). *I could love no one...until I loved me*. Phoenix, AZ: Perfect Bound Marketing.

Deutschman, A. (2008). *Change or die: The three keys to change at work and in life*. New York: Harper.

Dewey, C., & Dewey, C. (2016, November 18). Facebook fake-news writer: "I think Donald Trump is in the White House because of me." *The Washington Post*. Retrieved August 9, 2017, from http://www.highbeam.com/doc/1P2-40242841.html?refid=easy_hf

Eliot, T. S. (1943). *Four quartets*. Harcourt.

Emerson, R. W., & Emerson, E. W. (1903). *The complete works of Ralph Waldo Emerson; With a biographical introduction and notes*. Cambridge: Riverside Press.

Emerson, R. W. (1903) *Emerson's essay on compensation*. The University press of Sewanee, Tennessee. Retrieved December 27, 2017 from https://archive.org/stream/emersonsessayon00chasgoog#page/n2/mode/2up

Empower. (n.d.). In *Merriam-Webster's Dictionary* online. Retrieved August 08, 2017, from https://www.merriam-webster.com/dictionary/empower

Erker, S., PhD., & Thomas, B. Finding the first rung: A study on the challenges facing today's frontline leader (n.d.). Retrieved August 2,

2017, from http://www.ddiworld.com/ddi/media/trend-research/ findingthefirstrung_mis_ddi.pdf

Erker, S., PhD., & Thomas, B. (n.d.). Finding the first rung. Retrieved August 2, 2017, from http://www.ddiworld.com/ddi/media/trend-research

Feldman, G., Lian, H., Kosinski, M., & Stillwell, D. (2017). Frankly, we do give a damn. *Social Psychological and Personality Science,* 19485 5061668105. doi:10.1177/1948550616681055

Gladwell, M. (2013). *Outliers: The story of success.* New York: Back Bay Books.

Glaser, J. E. (2015, January 28). The neurochemistry of positive conversations. Retrieved August 09, 2017, from https://hbr.org/2014/06/the-neurochemistry-of-positive-conversations

Glossophobia.com. (n.d.). Retrieved October 12, 2017, from http://www.glossophobia.com/

Goewey, D. J. (2014). *The end of stress: Four steps to rewire your brain.* New York: Simon & Schuster.

Hall, K. (2010). *Aspire: Discover your purpose through the power of words.* New York: William Morrow.

Hawkins, D. R. (2011). *Power vs. force, the hidden determinants of human behavior: An anatomy of consciousness.* Sedona, AZ: Veritas.

Heimberg, R. G., Turk, C. L., & Mennin, D. S. (2004). *Generalized anxiety disorder: Advances in research and practice.* New York: Guilford Press.

Inf luence. (n.d.). In *Merriam-Webster's Dictionary* online. July 31, 2017, from https:// www.merriam-webster.com/dictionary/inf luence

Johnson, D. (2012, February 16). How much do useless meetings cost? Retrieved August 10, 2017, from http://www.cbsnews.com/news/how-much-do-useless-meetings-cost/

Karmen, A. (2016). *Crime victims: An introduction to victimology*. Boston, MA: Cengage Learning.

Manipulate. (n.d.). In *Merriam-Webster's Dictionary* online. Retrieved July 31, 2017, from https://www.merriam-webster.com/dictionary/manipulate

Meyers, N. (Director), Yuspa, C., Goldsmith, J., & Drake, D. (Writers), & Yuspa, C., & Goldsmith, J. (Screenwriters). (2000). *What women want* [Video file]. U.S.: Paramount.

News, C. (2017, April 16). Police: Suspect kills elderly victim on Facebook live, manhunt continues. Retrieved August 09, 2017, from https://www.cbsnews.com/news/cleveland-police-hunt-suspect-after-facebook-live-killing/

The power of praise and recognition. (2017, June 26). Retrieved October 12, 2017, from https://www.trainingjournal.com/articles/feature/power-praise-and-recognition

Pressfield, S. (2012). *The War of Art: Break Through the Blocks and Win Your Inner Creative Battles*. New York: Black Irish Entertainment.

The Pursuit of Happiness, Inc. (2016, September 10). Abraham Maslow. Retrieved October 11, 2017, from http://www.pursuit-of-happiness.org/history-of-happiness/abraham-maslow/

Rotna, R. (2008). Active learning. Retrieved August 02, 2017, from http://www.literacytrust.org.uk/

REFERENCES

Rozovsky, J. (2015, November 17). The five keys to a successful Google team. Retrieved October 02, 2017, from https://rework.withgoogle. com/blog/five-keys-to-a-successful-google-team/

Ruiz, M., & Wilton, N. (2012). *The four agreements: A practical guide to personal freedom.* San Rafael, CA: Amber-Allen.

Seventy-one percent of employers say they value emotional intelligence over IQ, according to CareerBuilder survey. (n.d.). Retrieved October 10, 2017, from http://www.careerbuilder.com/share/aboutus/ pressreleasesdetail.aspx?id=pr652&sd=8%2F18%2F2011&ed=08%2 F18%2F2011

Sinek, S. (2014). *Leaders eat last: Why some teams pull together and others don't.* Portfolio: Rep Rev edition.

Singh, G. (2010, July). How the world's IQ is in decline. Retrieved August, 2017. Cognitive Science Examiner.

Staff, A. (2013, December 12). 164.2 Billion Spent on Training and Development by U.S. Companies. Retrieved September 28, 2017, from https://www.td.org/Publications/Blogs/ATD-Blog/2013/12/ASTD-Releases-2013-State-of-the-Industry-Report

Staff, L. (2016, November 08). 10 facts: Abraham Lincoln and the gettysburg address. Retrieved August 01, 2017, from http://www.legacy. com/news/explore-history/article/10-facts-abraham-lincoln-and-the-gettysburg-address

Whitbourne, S. K. (2011, October 22). The essential guide to defense mechanisms. Retrieved August 08, 2017, from https://www.psychologytoday. com/blog/fulfillment-any-age/201110/the-essential-guide-defense-mechanisms

INDEX

4×4 pickup, 191–195, 217–218

A
abundance mindset, 22–24, 93
accountability
    in Art of Influencing Model, 172–173
    creating, 127–128
    pushback and, 135–138
    returning to owner of, 138–139
accountability partners, 85, 137–138
action plans, 170–171
adaptation, scarcity versus abundance mindset and, 24
advice, 92, 93
agendas, 200–201
Agile, 180
"Am I Enough" Syndrome, 41
amygdala, 99
anger, 136
Angoville-au-Plain, church in, 89–90
apologies, 206–207
application/point, 210–214
appreciation, 173–175
apprenticeships, 3–4
AQ (Awareness Quotient), 53
Arouet, François-Marie. *See* Voltaire
art, defined, 3
Art of Asking Questions. *See* questions
Art of Influencing Model
    overview, 163
    action plan creation, 170–171
    clarity of goals, 163–164
    commitment and accountability, 171–173
    cost identification, 168–169
    determining current position of self and other, 164–166
    journey of influence and, 175–176
    need identification, 167–168

235

obstacle identification, 169–170

wrapping up, 173–175

The Art of Leading Coaching & Influencing Others program, 4

Art of Presenting. *See* presentations

Aspire (Hall), 76

assessment, 43–47, 72–73

audience, knowledge of, 207–208

authenticity

answers to questions and, 63–64

defined, 63

facades and, 67–69

integrity and, 64–66

self-awareness and, 69

authority, 17–19

awareness. *See* self-awareness

Awareness Quotient (AQ), 53

B

Bandura, Albert, 39

Behavioral Assessment, 47

beliefs

coaching and, 103

ego and, 112–113

examining of, 69

as foundation of behaviors, 79–80

other-centered focus and, 187–188

re-beliefing of, 80–82

blame, 37

Bonnstetter, Ron, 46

book-endings, 220–221

bouncing back, 83–84

Branden, Nathaniel, 39

buy-in, 171, 183, 194–195, 207–210

buying versus selling, 164

C

call-backs, 218–219

challenging conversations

clarity about, 136–137

defense mechanism responses, 138–139

dis-ease addressed by, 132

need for, 133–134, 166

questions and, 99–100

role-play for, 137–138

trust and, 165

change, 79, 83–84, 143–144

Change or Die (Deutchsman), 83

choice

empowerment with, 127–129

questions to create, 123–126

church in Angoville-au-Plain, 89–90

Churchill, Winston, portrait of, 187

Coaching. *See also* questions; victim mentality

bad conversations as opportunity, 144

beliefs and, 103

cost of behavior, 134

defined, 60, 142–143

as empowerment, 129

examples of what is not, 91–92

fear and, 99

goal of, 144–145

gremlins and, 115–116

INDEX

leadership and, 93, 94, 142–143

long-term return on, 143–144

mindset and, 141–145

practice, 151

pushback to, 135–138

ten things to remember, forget, and do, 147–150

Coaching Quotient (CQ), 96

commitment, 171–173

communication difficulties, 29, 97–98

communication style, 25–28

compare/contrast, 189–190, 191, 214–216

compartmentalization of selves, 64–66

compensation law, 27, 168

conflict, cultural background and, 21

confusion as defense, 135–136

Congressman facade, 67

consequences, 37

contrast/compare, 189–190, 191, 214–216

Contreras, Joe, 41

control, 19, 158. *See also* power versus force

costs, 168–169

CQ (Coaching Quotient), 96

crying, 135–136

cutting losses, 175

D

David sculpture, 1–3, 223, 227

decision making, 23–24, 115

defense mechanisms, 133, 135–136, 138–139

deflection, 135

delegation, trust and, 25

denial, 51

Deutschman, Alan, 83

Development Dimensions International Inc. survey, 30

di Duccio, Agostino, 1

dictators, 19

difficult conversations. *See* challenging conversations

dis-ease, 134. *See also* coaching

Do You See Me facade, 67

domestication process of people, 40

dragons, 136

drama, emotional, 115–116, 120. *See also* victim mentality

dumbing down, 135–136

E

ego, 158

Ego in Fear F.I.L.L.E.R.S.™ Process, 112–113

Einstein, Albert, 21

Einstein facade, 67

Eliot, T. S., 168, 175, 220–221

emotional connection with audience, 208–214, 217–218

emotional drama, 115–116, 120. *See also* victim mentality

Emotional Intelligence (EQ), 44–47, 178

employee-based locus-of-control, 32

empowerment, 95, 127–129

The End of Stress (Goeway), 109
engagement, 31–33, 99–100
enough, being, 38–42, 67–69, 112
entitlement, 27, 30–31
EQ (Emotional Intelligence), 44–47, 178
Everett, Edward, 17
excuses. *See* defense mechanisms; victim mentality
executive functions, 99
extraordinary leaders. *See* leaders; leadership
extrapolation/magnification, 190–191, 216–217
extroverts, 35

F
facades, 64–69, 113
facilitation
  overview, 177
  defined, 60
  explained, 177–179
  to increase buy-in, 194–195
  other-centered versus self-centered focus and, 184–185
  process of, 179–184
fake news, 155–156
faux agreement, 136
faux productivity, 199–200
fear. *See also* gremlins
  benefits of, 114–115
  coaching and, 99
  consequences of, 58–59
  forward movement and, 114–115

goals and, 117
loss as basis of, 110–111
power versus force and, 24–25
rational assessment of, 114
unsubstantiated, 109–110
worldview and, 21–22
Fear F.I.L.L.E.R.S.™ Process, 111–115
feedback. *See* Outside-In path to self-awareness
A Few Good Men, 26
fight or flight, 99. *See also* fear
fit to job, 75
focus, 19, 20. *See also* other-centered focus; self-centered focus
Fonda, Henry, 109
force, 15, 19. *See also* power versus force
forward movement, 13, 75, 114–115
The Four Agreements (Ruiz), 40
Four Quartets (Eliot), 168
4×4 pickup, 191–195, 217–218
freebies, 27
freedom in Fear F.I.L.L.E.R.S.™ Process, 111

G
Gallup, 72–73
generational differences, 33, 167
Gettysburg Address, 17
Gibson, Mel, 108
Gladwell, Malcolm, 139
glorified individual contributors (GIC)
  example of, 55

INDEX

micromanagement by, 56, 57
quiz to determine, 59–61
glossophobia, 205. *See also* presentations; public speaking
goals, fear and, 117
Godwin, Robert, Sr. shooting, 155
Goeway, Don Joseph, 109
gremlins, 107, 108–110, 115–116

H

habits, changing, 143–144
Hall, Kevin, 76
Hawkins, David, 16
Heckler, Lou, 219
Hierarchy of Needs, 111–114
honesty, integrity and, 66
Horner, Paul, 156
humor, 218

I

I Could Love No One Until I Loved Me (Contreras), 41
impatience, 158
Imposter facade, 67
Income in Fear F.I.L.L.E.R.S.™ Process, 111–112
individual contributors, 11, 30, 56–57. *See also* glorified individual contributors (GIC)
influence. *See also* Art of Influencing Model; painting their picture
defined, 11–12, 157
factors affecting, 158
inside-out, 159–161

intention and, 157–158
journey of, 175–176
leadership and, 10–11, 12–14
listening versus answering questions and, 28–29
manipulation compared, 12, 155–156, 157
outside-in, 159
power and, 17–19
practice, 176
quiz to determine intentions, 161–162
as soft skill, 4
Influence Quotient (InQ), 33
Inside-Out path to self-awareness, 44, 50–53, 159–161
integration of selves, 64–66
integrity, authenticity and, 64–66
intentions. *See* influence; manipulation
introverts, 35

J

Jesus, influence of, 17
judgment, 123

L

Law of Compensation, 27, 168
Law of Motion, 15, 19
Law of Reciprocity, 66, 121–122
leader-based locus-of-control, 32
leaders
apprenticeships lacking for, 3–4

defined, 55

jump from individual contributors to, 56–57

as pathfinders, 76

quiz to identify, 59–61

reason for becoming, 77–78, 84–85

supervisors compared, 160

Leaders Eat Last: Why Some Teams Pull Together and Others Don't (Sinek), 173–174

leadership

being responsible for, 36

coaching and, 93, 94, 142–143

comparison of good and bad, 223–225

defined, 10–11

desire lacking for, 51–52

emotional intelligence and, 45–46

fear and, 58–59

influence and, 12–14

manipulation compared, 156

meeting culture and, 202–203

quasi-leaders compared, 56–57

skill changes needed for, 56

strengths and, 71–76

trust as cornerstone of, 156

your own story for, 227–228

lean technology, 45–46

letting go, 59, 175

leveraging people, 178. *See also* facilitation

lies by omission, 26

Life in Fear F.I.L.L.E.R.S.™ Process, 112

Lincoln, Abraham, 17

listening, 28–29, 97–98, 207

locus-of-control, 18 19, 31 33, 160

loss, as basis of fear, 110–111

Love in Fear F.I.L.L.E.R.S.™ Process, 112

M

magnification/extrapolation, 190–191

manipulation

influence compared, 12, 155–156, 157

leadership compared, 156

opaque communication style as, 26

Marine Corps, 33

masks, 113

Maslow's Hierarchy of Needs, 111–114

meetings. *See also* facilitation

laws of conducting, 200–203

as productivity drains, 197–200

purpose statements for, 180–181

Michelangelo's *David* sculpture, 1–3, 223, 227

micromanagement

control versus power and, 19

fear as basis for, 58

glorified individual contributors and, 56, 57

trust and, 25

INDEX

millennials, 33
mirrors, 122–123. *See also* painting
 their picture
mistakes, 206–207
Moore, Kenneth, 89
Mr./Mrs. Never Enough facade, 67

N

Newton's Third Law of Motion, 15,
 19
Nicholson, Jack, 26
normal, perception of, 21
not enough mentality, 38–42, 67–69,
 112

O

objective feedback. *See* Outside-In
 path to self-awareness
obstacles, 41–42, 68, 94–95. *See also*
 mirrors; painting their picture
off-color humor, 218
opaque communication style, 25–28
opinions, 187–188
other-awareness, 137
other-centered focus
 overview, 19–20
 beliefs and, 187–188
 coaching and, 115–116, 142
 facilitation and, 184–185
 influence as, 157
 leadership and, 12–14
 presentations and, 206
 quiz to determine, 161–162
 responsibility and, 37

Outlier (Gladwell), 139
Outside-In path to self-awareness
 overview, 43–44
 influence and, 159
 objective feedback for, 44–47
 subjective feedback, 47–50
owning yourself, 35–42

P

painting their picture
 4×4 pickup, 191–195
 compare/contrast for, 189–190,
 191
 magnification/extrapolation for,
 190–191
 purposes of, 188–189
 Winston Churchill example of,
 187–188
pathfinders, 76
patience, 1–3
pauses, 219–220
perfection, 37–38
personal inventory, 47
pivot points, 213–214
plan-awareness, 137
play bigger. *See* coaching
point/application, 210–214
power, 19. *See also* empowerment
power versus force
 overview, 15–16
 asking versus telling and, 28–29
 authority and, 17–19
 coaching and, 142–143
 communication style and, 25–28

focus and, 19–20

jump to leadership and, 58

locus-of-control and, 31–33

resource mentality and, 22–24

self-assessment of, 33

trust or fear as driver and, 24–25

view of, 21–22, 30–31

Power vs. Force (Hawkins), 16

practice, 139, 151

praise, 173–175

presentations

4×4 pickup for, 217–218

book-endings in, 220–221

buy-in for, 207–210

call-backs in, 218–219

compare/contrast for, 214–216

defined, 60

emotional connection with audience, 208–214, 217–218

extrapolation/magnification for, 216–217

humor in, 218

pauses in, 219–220

practice for, 222

as privilege, 221

purpose of, 205

reasons for audience to listen, 207

storytelling and, 210–214

privilege, power versus force and, 30–31

Procrastinator facade, 67

productivity, meetings and, 197–200

profanity, 63–64, 218

projection, 47–48, 133

psychological safety, 32

public speaking, 177–178. *See also* facilitation; presentations

purpose statements, 180–181, 200–203

pushback, 135–138

Q

quasi-leaders and contributors, 56–57

Qubein, Nido, 115

questions

benefits of, 104–105, 132

to create choice, 123–126

decision making and, 115

feedback requests and, 49–50

future-based, 167

importance of, 94–95, 166

inauthentic responses to, 63–64

open and general, 102–103

pacing of, 100

poor style with, 100–102

power and force and, 28–29

progression of, 103

strength utilization and, 73–74

talking versus, 97–98

third person questions, 116

tone for, 139

R

reaping what you sow, 121–122

re-believing, 80–82

reciprocity, 121–122

recognition, 174

redirection, 135

relationship building, 48

reptilian brain, 99

Reputation in Fear F.I.L.L.E.R.S.™ Process, 113

resistance. *See* gremlins

resource mentality, 22–24

responsibility. *See also* victim mentality

    other-centered focus and, 19–20, 37

    for self, 35–42

right, need to be, 132–133, 141–142

risk, 23, 115

role-play, 137–138

Rossellino, Antonio, 1

Ruiz, Don Miguel, 40

rules for engagement, 201–202

S

safety, 144

Salsbury, Glenna, 211

sarcasm, 218

scalability, 31, 57

scarcity mindset, 22–24, 93

Security in Fear F.I.L.L.E.R.S.™ Process, 113–114

self-awareness

    overview, 43–44

    authenticity and, 69

    Awareness Quotient and, 53

    challenging conversations and, 137

    changing based on feedback about, 50

    inventory for, 47

    "not enough" mentality and, 68–69

    objective feedback for, 44–47

    self-reflection for, 50–53

    subjective feedback for, 47–50

    symptoms of lack of, 52

self-centered focus

    overview, 19–20

    coaching and, 115–116

    facilitation and, 184–185

    manipulation as, 157

    presentations and, 206

    quiz to determine, 161–162

    responsibility and, 37

self-deprecating humor, 218

self-efficacy, 39–40

self-esteem, 39–40

self-fulfilling prophecies, 79

self-protection, 21–22

self-reflection. *See* Inside-Out path to self-awareness

self-worth, 39–40

selling versus buying, 164

shutting down, 136

Sinek, Simon, 173–174

The Six Pillars of Self-Esteem (Branden), 39

soft skills, 4. *See also* Emotional Intelligence (EQ)

S.P.A. formula, 211–214, 222

speaking, power and force and, 28–29

Starfish story, 211

storytelling, 210–214

strengths, 71–76

StrengthsFinder 2.0 book, 72–73

StrengthsFinder® Assessment, 72–73
stress, 52, 72
struggle, 9
supervisors, leaders compared, 160
support, 172–173
Sustaining Change Model, 79, 182.
  See also beliefs
Sutherland, Graham, 187

T
talent loss, 57
Target Training International (TTI),
  45, 46
telephone message game, 29, 98
ten things to remember, forget, and
  do, 147–150
thanks, 174
Third Law of Motion, 15, 19
third person questions, 116
timing, 219–220
training, 4, 30, 78
transparent communication style,
  25–28
trust
  challenging conversations and,
    165
  feedback and, 48
  focus and, 19, 20
  leadership and, 156
  power versus force and, 24–25
  scalability and, 31
  self-protection versus, 21–22
  transparency versus opaque-
    ness and, 28

vulnerability and, 144
  in who you are, 68–69
truth, 26–27
TTI (Target Training International),
  45, 46

U
United State Marine Corps, 33
Universal Law of Compensation,
  27, 168
Universal Law of Reciprocity,
  121–122

V
value, feedback and, 48
victim mentality
  overview, 119–122
  choice creation for, 123–126
  empowerment and, 127–129
  holding mirror up and, 122–123
  prevalence of, 37
  rewards from, 121
victimology, 120
Voltaire, 29, 97–98
vulnerability, 192–193

W
Waterfall, 180
Wells Fargo fake accounts, 226–227
What Women Want, 108
Winston Churchill portrait, 187
Wizard of Oz, 68–69
worldview, 21–22
Wright, Robert, 89–90

ACKNOWLEDGEMENTS

I want to thank every one of my clients, who, over the years, have helped me to develop, shape, and reshape the concepts that are presented in this book.

I have been fortunate to have some amazing mentors in my life whom I've had the privilege of walking beside for all of these years guiding me along the way.

Someone once said, "Your family is chosen for you and you choose your friends."

I have been so fortunate in both of these areas. Both friends and family living and deceased have guided me in so many ways through this journey I call life. Words can never express the gratitude I feel so I will not even attempt to try to explain or describe.

Thank you to my editor Kelly Lydick, who helped shape this material into a finished package, and David Moratto, who captured the essence of this book in both the cover and the internal layout.

I used to think people were either good or bad, but the longer I live, I realize that folks are either conscious and awake or unconscious and asleep. Either way, there is always something to learn from either one, if I am willing to look for the good in all people and trust that what is unfolding in this moment, it is exactly as it supposed to be.